How clean is your house?

How clean
is your house?

Kim Woodburn and Aggie MacKenzie

PENGUIN BOOKS

For Mum, my all-time cleaning guru.
And Rory and Ewan, who keep me in
constant practice. **Aggie**

For my Pete, the day I met you all my
birthdays came at once. **Kim**

PENGUIN BOOKS

Published by the Penguin Group
Penguin Books Ltd, 80 Strand, London WC2R 0RL, England
Penguin Group (USA) Inc., 375 Hudson Street, New York, New York 10014, USA
Penguin Books Australia Ltd, 250 Camberwell Road, Camberwell, Victoria 3124, Australia
Penguin Books Canada Ltd, 10 Alcorn Avenue, Toronto, Ontario, Canada M4V 3B2
Penguin Books India (P) Ltd, 11 Community Centre,
Panchsheel Park, New Delhi – 110 017, India
Penguin Books (NZ) Ltd, Cnr Airborne and Rosedale Roads,
Albany, Auckland, New Zealand
Penguin Books (South Africa) (Pty) Ltd, 24 Sturdee Avenue,
Rosebank 2196, South Africa

Penguin Books Ltd, Registered Offices: 80 Strand, London WC2R 0RL, England

www.penguin.com

First published by Michael Joseph 2003
Published in Penguin Books 2004
1

Copyright © Talkback, 2003

The moral right of the authors has been asserted

Set in Thesis Sans and New Clarendon
Designed and typeset by Smith & Gilmour, UK
Photography: Mark Read
Project Editor: Gillian Haslam
Printed in Italy by Graphicom srl

A CIP catalogue record for this book is available from the British Library

Contents

Aggie MacKenzie

You'd probably like to know a little bit more about the two stars of *How Clean Is Your House?*, wouldn't you? The tall, busty, rather fierce woman with the striking blonde retro hairstyle, famed for her twinsets, pearls and decorous rubber gloves, and the wee (by comparison) Scot who's always poking immaculately manicured fingernails into filthy nooks and crannies looking for beasties and bacteria.

Aggie was born in Rothiemurchus, near Aviemore, Scotland. At Kingussie High School, she discovered an aptitude for languages. 'I can say "filth" in German, French, Italian and even Latin!' Aggie was taught the art of cleaning by her mother, who deployed a dizzying array of remedies for spots and stains.

Aggie studied for a bilingual secretarial qualification in Aberdeen, then came to London to work at the Foreign Office. 'On my first day they told me I had been security-screened and I would actually be working for MI6!' She hadn't quite envisaged a career as Miss Moneypenny, and after two years of high-level secrets crossing her desk (she won't tell you, so don't ask) she left to join the press office of the National Union of Students. It was there that she got a call from her older sister Kerry, who was a journalist working on Woman's World. Aggie's career in magazines now began in earnest, working on a string of national titles, before arriving at Good Housekeeping as associate editor in charge of the Good Housekeeping Institute, which is where they test all the latest consumer appliances, develop and test recipes and investigate new cleaning products and gadgets.

In August 2002 Aggie was asked if she would like to be considered for a TV series. At the screen test she was introduced to a rather scary lady called Kim. 'I'd never met anyone like her,' Aggie remembers fondly. Kim and Aggie were asked to comment on and clean a researcher's grimy flat. It was, of course, the birth of 'The Nation's Dream Cleaning Team'.

Aggie lives in London with her architect husband Matthew and sons Rory, 12, and Ewan, 8. 'After each show Ewan appears wearing rubber gloves and asks, "Mum, can we clean now?"' The highlight for her so far was appearing on *V Graham Norton*: 'Rory thought it was the height of cool. Kim and I had our own dressing-rooms and a gift with a note from our host, saying, "Many thanks and lots of wet kisses." You don't get that at the houses we visit!' When Aggie's not working, cleaning or tending her allotment, she adores cooking. 'On my day off, I could happily bake all day long.'

Kim Woodburn

Kim was born in Eastney, near Portsmouth. She first noticed the joy of cleaning while watching her fastidious grandmother, who cleaned schools for a living, soaking clothes, scrubbing the step and polishing like crazy. 'She sparkled,' exclaims Kim. However, Kim's first job after leaving school at 15 was in a high-class fashion shop, ironing the clothes that would be displayed in the window.

She took up her first live-in cleaning job after moving to Liverpool, cleaning 'from breakfast time until the end of time'. A variety of jobs followed: at a toy factory, a holiday camp, as a beautician, a social worker, even a model in the Littlewoods catalogue.

Kim also started knitting, and founded a handmade knitwear company. As a tall lady, with a, shall we say, bigger than average bust, she couldn't get anything other than frumpy cardies to fit, so she started her own range. In 1983 Kim made her television debut modelling her range on *Pebble Mill At One*, with Jeff Banks. It was 20 years before television would rediscover Kim Woodburn.

In 1979 Kim married her husband, Peter. They are so inseparable that they decided to give up their shift working (he was a policeman) and moved to America, where they kept house for the rich and famous. They returned to Britain eight years ago and currently look after a sheik and his holiday home in Kent.

Before the *How Clean is Your House?* screen test, Kim was told she would be meeting someone called Aggie. 'I thought she was the presenter and I was the cleaner!' Kim recalls saying to the girl whose filthy flat it was: 'You're 26, but you won't see 30 living in all this muck and filth.' Needless to say she got the job on the spot.

When asked if she has ever employed a cleaner herself, Kim isn't impressed, 'Don't insult me!' When she leaves her home in Pembrokeshire to go and care for the sheik, Kim covers everything in plastic and vacuums herself out of the door. Asked if she isn't just a tiny bit obsessive about cleaning, she replies, 'I don't worry about being called obsessive, as long as I'm clean, I'm happy – and I'm having the time of my life!'

Are you a filth offender?

You might wonder exactly how clean we're all supposed to be. Surely no one can live up to our exacting standards? You're certain you're not as filthy as the mucky people we visit on the show, but perhaps you've got the odd nook and cranny you'd rather we didn't poke our fingers into on a surprise visit?

Before you read this book we think it would be a good thing for you to discover whether you are a filth offender and how much your home resembles a grime scene. Make an honest note of your score – no cheating, you mucky puppies!

Which of the following statements best describes your approach to cleaning?
A   A little each day is the best way.
B   I do it when it looks like a tip.
C   I don't really have time.
D   It's something other people do.

When is vacuuming best done?
A   Before breakfast.
B   Once a week.
C   Only when expecting visitors.
D   Do we own a vacuum cleaner?

How often do you do the washing up?
A   Immediately anything gets used.
B   Definitely at the end of every day.
C   When the sink starts to overflow with dirty dishes.
D   When there isn't any clean crockery left.

How frequently do you change/wash the cloth you wipe kitchen surfaces with?
A   Every day.
B   Once a week.
C   Not very often.
D   I can't honestly remember.

When was the last time you defrosted the freezer?
A   I have a frost-free model and wipe down regularly.
B   Usually when there's more ice than food.
C   When the door wouldn't shut anymore.
D   Not in the last three years.

Quentin Crisp famously said that dust doesn't get worse after four years.
A   But dusting is therapeutic!
B   A quick flick round with the duster never hurts.
C   That's excessive, but certainly six months doesn't show up much.
D   I couldn't agree more.

Who's been sleeping in your bed (with you)?
Dust mites love dirty sheets. How often do you
wash yours?

A Once a week.

B Once a fortnight.

C About once a month.

D I can't quite remember. Ask me another.

How clean is your toilet?

A I could eat my dinner off it.

B I swish a brush around and squirt bleach
down it once a week.

C It's always other people who leave it murky

D Well, I flush it when I use it.

Getting back to normal after a big party involves

A Staying up late and getting everything spick
and span for the morning.

B Enjoying myself and worrying about it in the
morning.

C You can't really tell the difference from normal.

D People rarely come to visit much anymore.

When visitors are calling, do you

A Do nothing, everything is already spotless.

B Throw the vacuum round quickly

C Apologise in advance about the mess.

D See answer D, left.

Your cleaning profile

Mostly As

You are a cleaning queen! We are chuffed with you,
aren't we Ags? It's so heartwarming to find a soul
mate after all the filth we've had to endure recently.
We can just see you now, dusting, polishing, scouring
and scrubbing your pristine home, with your gloves
always at the ready. You're going to love trying out
all our wonderful tips.

Mostly Bs

It's never any fun being average, is it? Who wants to
be the middle of the road? Go on dear, try and better
yourself. Don't show the world your slovenly ways,
best foot forward, let yourself sparkle, you'll feel
better for it!

Mostly Cs

It's the slippery slope for you, my dear. A dirty, grimy
home is nothing to be proud of. Any more filth and
your bed sheets will be walking themselves to the
washing machine for a good soak. Oh we can't
abide laziness, can we Ags?

Mostly Ds

You are a filth offender. You filthy, dirty beggar.
It's not clever, so wipe that smirk off your face. If
you don't mend your ways you won't see your next
birthday living in that hole. Failing that, you'd better
write to us and we'll be round to sort you out,
won't we Ags?

How clean is your house?

We really have had a lot of fun cleaning up Britain, and getting Britain cleaning. We've travelled from Brighton to Glasgow, with many stops in between, and filth doesn't vary much, you know. Whether you're poor or posh, young or old, if you don't clean you'll end up in a terrible state. Oh, but we've met some wonderful people, dirty mucky people, but lovely all the same. The poor souls, their homes had got completely out of control.

We loved cleaning them up, getting inside all their nooks and crannies and dislodging decades of ingrained muck. We left surfaces gleaming, taps shining, carpets spotless, beds fresh and baths fit for an emperor. The amazing thing is that it wasn't only the people we visited who started cleaning – you've been telling us that after the show you've suddenly felt the urge to put on the rubber gloves and get scrubbing too! Oh, we're so thrilled you're turning into a nation of cleaning queens!

You've stopped us in the street and told us how much you love the tips we dispense, and you've asked how you can get your taps de-scaled, or get the marks off your sofa, or get the bath to gleam again, and how to get rid of the smell in the fridge. 'Can you write down your fabulous cleaning tips?' you've begged us.

So we're very pleased to share them with you here. We've packed these pages with the answers to your questions, the tips we used in the series, and much more. We hope that you'll dip in and out of the book whenever you're faced with a new cleaning challenge, and that your homes will thank you for it.

People ask us what we like so much about cleaning. What is there not to like? The pleasure that relaxing in a clean and fresh home brings is so satisfying. Less mess, more rest, is what we say … knowing that everything is in its place should we need it, that the cushions are plumped, the bed is fresh, the washing up is done and the floors are clean. You may well blush: if you're thinking to yourself that sounds like hard work, you're doing something wrong, dear. It only takes a few minutes a day to keep everything straight. Trust us – we can show you that domesticity needn't be drudgery. So what are you waiting for? Let's get cleaning!

Getting started

Kim and Aggie's essential cleaning kit

A glance at the shelves of cleaning materials in any large store will tell you that there is a breathtaking array of cleaning creams, powders, polishes, liquids, cloths, mops and tablets available. Of course you don't need them all! Some are time-saving, but buying so many products is hardly economical – we'll show you other cleaning methods that avoid buying a special product which does only one job. However, every home should have a basic cleaning kit. All the homes we visited contained cleaning materials – they just weren't being used. Their purchase was a sign of the best intentions, but then they had been buried at the back of a cupboard – often covered in grease or dust!

Name a product and you can be sure that we have tried it. Here is a list of the supplies we never set off without when we take to the road to clean up Britain's filthiest homes. These will work in your home too – even if you have a lot less grime.

Kim

I've got a tried and tested collection of cleaning materials which I always turn to whenever there's a job to be done. I like a nice collection of dusters, cloths and mops – we all have our favourites, don't we dear? But these work for me, so I have no hesitation recommending them to you.

Washing and scrubbing

Washing-up liquid – don't economize – the concentrated stuff is best. Good for your dishes, your floors, your walls – you name it, washing-up liquid can often do it. Hot soapy water is a clear winner for hundreds of tasks.

Scouring powder – I swear by a strong abrasive powder with coarse grit particles for the toughest of cleaning jobs. You can't use it on every surface – especially not plastic, because you'll soon rub all the shine off. But scouring powder is perfect for scrubbing inside the toilet pan, for example.

Cream cleaner – this is good for more delicate surfaces that won't take a coarse grit powder, such as plastic baths. It's good on grease and very useful in the kitchen and bathroom.

Soap-filled wire pads – or just the plain wire or nylon pads for jobs where you don't want huge amounts of soap swishing about, just a good bit of elbow grease. They can be used carefully on some cookers to remove spills on the hob, and inside the oven too. Roasting tins are a beggar, aren't they? Good for a few months, then you get a build-up of brown spots.

Washing soda crystals – a good old-fashioned cleaning product, with a whole host of uses. Great for washing down surfaces and especially good at cutting through grease. They are also a very powerful weapon in the battle against slimy and smelly drains. Used regularly they can save you an expensive call to a specialist drain-cleaning company. Mix with a small amount of very hot water and pour down the sink, or directly into the outside drain to help keep them clear.

Bleach – don't over-use bleach, it's really not necessary. Warm soapy water will often do, but a little dash of bleach in your bucket of soapy water will make some tough jobs easier.

Distilled white vinegar – another wonderful traditional remedy my mother used which is just as good today. Use it for removing limescale – but not on plated surfaces or it will remove the plating too. Wash off thoroughly after use. It's how my mother cleaned filthy windows – one part vinegar, nine parts water. But the solution needs to be rubbed off firmly with old newspaper or it can leave smears. A little vinegar is also good for pet urine on carpet, and it deters pets from returning to the same spot.

Toilet soap – wonderful, but not in guest bathrooms. Who wants to use someone else's old soap? Liquid soap dispensers are best for guests. Rub a damp face cloth over soap to tackle all manner of marks – such as lipstick on a shirt collar or a cotton sweater. Don't rub heavily or you'll spoil the weave.

Liquid carpet shampoo spray – I swear by this for small marks, but use it as soon as they appear. Test a small hidden area first to ensure it won't spoil the carpet colour, and leave for at least half an hour. For small marks just rub your fingernail along with the pile and tease through the soap. Bang with a damp cloth, followed by a dry cloth. Dirty carpets should be professionally cleaned, and don't be stingy with expensive rugs – take them to a specialist cleaner. If you could afford to buy the rugs you can afford to have them cleaned.

Dishwasher liquid – not only good in the dishwasher, but also for cleaning plastic baths. Don't let dirt build up or you may mark the plastic permanently.

Biological washing powder – not only is this great in your washing machine, it's also very good for cleaning a dirty bath. Fill the bath with warm water, add a couple of cups of powder, and leave to soak overnight. (You can even add men's dirty white shirts and do two jobs at once.) Rinse and buff dry.

Fabric conditioner – a wonderful invention. Choose your favourite fragrance. It's very good on natural fibres, but not on your bathing suits, they really don't like it.

Denture-cleaning tablets – these will clean more than just your false teeth! Pop one down the loo for a sparkling pan, or even dissolve a couple in the kettle overnight. They will loosen the limescale and you can wipe it off with paper towel in the morning. Rinse after use – who wants to drink tea made with denture tablets?

getting started

It's called
elbow
grease!

Gloves, mops, cloths and other useful weapons in the fight against grime

Gloves – I like black rubber gloves best, and I love the novelty designs you can get now. Buy them a size too big, they're much more comfortable. You can even wear a pair of cotton gloves inside, soaked with hand cream to keep your hands moisturized and soft all day.

Toothbrushes – these are invaluable. Save every one! Never throw your old ones away, simply put them to a new use. They are perfect for getting into any little crevice that your fingers won't fit, or wouldn't want to.

Cotton wool buds – these are similarly useful, especially for delicate items like computer keyboards.

Cocktail sticks – if you're as fussy as I am, these are perfect for picking dirt out of screw heads.

String mops – my chosen weapon for dirty floors. They're tough, absorb a lot of water, and bleach beautifully. You can wring them out really tight to stop the floor getting too wet. Change the water frequently, and never leave a mop head dirty. Wash it out thoroughly, and never leave it sitting in a bucket – oh, the pong – stand it head upright to dry.

Dusters and rags – why do they make dusters in such bright colours? They are only any good when the dye is washed out. Buy a dozen the same colour and put them straight into the washing machine or soak them. Go through the agony – it's worth it. Have a good supply of old white towels and rags (keep your old vests and T-shirts) – not coloured, mind, you don't want to transfer the dye to something you're cleaning, especially a carpet.

Chamois leathers – my first choice for polishing windows after washing with a soapy solution. They work on the small panes beautifully, and well cared for they last for years.

Vacuum cleaner – I like an upright. Why break your back? You can get hose attachments, too, for reaching right up to ceilings, and the brushes work wonders on upholstery and dusty furniture. Better to pick the dust up than swish it round. I like the bagless cleaners with the clear drums – watching all that dirt spin around is free entertainment. At first you think to yourself, this room isn't so dirty, and then you are amazed just how much dust you've managed to find when you see it spinning round. When I go away I like to vacuum myself out of the front door, so it's all nice and fresh for my return.

Polishing

Spray furniture polish – you can get some lovely fragrances. Don't over-use, though, or your furniture will get polish-bound. Once a month is plenty, the rest of the time dust with a very slightly damp duster, wrung out as tight as you can. Finally, buff with a dry duster.

Beeswax polish – wonderful on rough and unpolished woods, such as pine tables. You can see when wood is gasping for some nourishment. Rub it in well and buff up with a lint-free cloth – men's old vests (washed, of course, and not the string ones) are perfect.

Cream pads for silver – but use gloves. A silver cloth is good, but expensive. A good tip for cleaning silver items, not plate, mind, but good for your jewellery. Line a plastic bowl with aluminium foil, shiny side up, and add a handful of soda crystals and some very hot water. Put your silver in for 1–5 minutes – watch the dirt jump to the foil and the silver emerge sparkling. Rinse thoroughly and buff with a dry cloth.

Spray lubricant (WD40) – often found in the garage, but useful all round the home. Great for getting paint off windows – give a quick spray to loosen it, then apply a plastic scraper and elbow grease. Ensure the room is well ventilated.

Aggie

I have quite a short list. I don't like the clutter of having cupboards full of stuff when just a few products can tackle so many jobs. I also worry about the effects on the environment of using so many unnecessary chemicals. But these are the things I do like.

Washing and scrubbing

Washing-up liquid – I love this, especially the concentrated stuff. It can do so many jobs, even removing all sorts of stains from kids' clothes. Squirt some on to the stain, grab the surrounding fabric with both hands and rub well, then stuff into the washing machine. Washing-up liquid is good for so many household surfaces, and a little really does go a long way.

Cream cleaner – this has an abrasive action. I prefer it to the powder scourers, because I worry about breathing in the airborne particles.

Bleach – I prefer the really thick stuff, which is less likely to splash on your clothes and ruin them. I've had too many accidents! I like the way it clings to the sides of the loo rather than disappearing straight down the pan.

Bicarbonate of soda – a good alternative to detergent if you suffer from allergies or are sensitive to chemicals. It's great on stainless steel, it's good for sinks, it's even good sprinkled into smelly trainers, and it's kind to the environment. My homemade scouring mix is a winner: add bicarbonate of soda to bleach to form a paste. This is very good at removing soap scum from shower tiles when rubbed on with a nylon pad (in general you should not mix cleaning products, as they can cause dangerous gases and reactions, but this tip, like all our tips, is tried and tested).

Washing soda – this is great at removing grease. I fill my butler's sink overflow with it, then pour over a kettle of boiling water and have a little scrub with a bottle brush to get rid of any grimy bits. It's good down the plughole once a month too, to stop build-up of grease which can block drains.

Biological washing powder – I prefer the powder to the tablets, which are expensive and so fiddly to open. It's easier to gauge a good scoop of powder to the level of dirt and size of the load. Here's my top tip for cleaning your roasting tins using washing powder. No need to scrub. Sprinkle in a cup full of powder, add warm water, and leave to soak for an hour or so. If it's really bad, put the roasting tin, plus solution, on the hob, heat gently for about 10 minutes, then wash as normal.

Trigger cleaning sprays – I like these in the bathroom because they are quick and easy to use. I apply the spray to the bath and basin and leave it to work its magic while I clean the tiles.

Distilled white vinegar – Kim and I never leave for a job without this. It's good on limescale, for wiping down your shower door, and it's great on mirrors. After washing windows with a warm soapy water solution, buff up with vinegar and kitchen towel.

Gloves, cloths and other useful weapons in the fight against grime

Gloves – keep separate gloves for bathroom and kitchen to prevent transfer of bacteria. Kim and I detest toilet brushes, so gloves on and down the pan is the only real way to clean. After all, who wants a minging brush sitting around?

Dishcloths – the only kind for me are those cotton ones with red stitched edging. They should be washed every day – either in the washing machine with the white wash, or in the dishwasher with the plates. Alternatively, at the end of the day you can soak them in warm soapy water with a few drops of bleach added – good for the sink, too.

Tea towels – I prefer linen glass cloths. They should be ironed and folded. A hot iron also helps to sterilize them. Always use a separate hand towel in the kitchen.

Lambswool dusters – I like these very much. They act like a magnet to dust, so you know it's not just being flicked around the room.

Toothbrushes – these are excellent for scrubbing dirty grouting between tiles. One part bleach, one part water, about once every couple of months, will keep everything sparkling white.

Paint scrapers – I like to use these on the glass of the oven door. If yours is removable glass like mine, unscrew it, give it a good soak in hot soapy water, and then use the scraper to shift any stuck-on grease marks. It's also a good idea every so often to pull out free-standing kitchen appliances and get to work with the scraper on any little bits of food debris clinging to the sides of the units and appliances. It comes off really quickly!

Vacuum cleaner – I like a bagless cylinder model, as I am quite short and find it much easier to carry upstairs than an upright. I'm not keen on bags, as they are expensive and wasteful and a faff to buy.

Polishes

Beeswax polish – I don't like spray polishes at all; again, I worry about ingesting those airborne particles. I prefer creams or solid blocks. These are great on wood – on with one cloth, buff with another. Once a month is plenty – you don't want your lovely furniture to get polish-bound.

Salt and lemon juice – three parts salt to one part lemon juice. This works really well on copper and brass. Rinse and buff dry with a soft cloth.

Spray lubricant (WD40) – this is very good at removing the stickers your kids plant all over their bedroom doors. Peel off the top layer, then spray the residue, wipe with a kitchen towel and hey presto, it's gone (if the stickers have been in place a long time you might need a plastic scraper to ease the way).

getting started

If you spend two evenings cleaning, that's still five nights off

Grime scene pests

DIRT DETECTIVE AGGIE'S
MOST UNWANTED GRIME FILE

'There is no need to do any housework at all. After the first four years the dirt doesn't get any worse. It is simply a matter of not losing one's nerve.' Quentin Crisp

We lost count of the number of people who repeated this famous quote to us when we visited their filthy, dirty homes.

The truth is that if you are a filth offender there are plenty of pests that will very happily come and live with you in your squalor. They spread bacteria and germs which can cause poisoning, allergies and illness – such as salmonella, asthma and dysentery.

Using my dirt detective sample bags and swabs I apprehended plenty of villains lurking in the grime scenes we inspected. If you find your home overrun with any of these pests you know it's time to get cleaning.

Dust mites

Modern, warm, humid homes provide ideal conditions for dust mites. They especially love living in our beds, which are warm and moist.

They feed on flakes of human skin – we each shed about 1 gram every day. They go to the toilet often and their faeces contain harmful enzymes.

Up to 30 per cent of the population suffers from asthma, eczema, bronchitis or itchy eyes caused by dust mite faeces.

Fortunately dust mites can only be seen under the microscope – if you could see the ugly brutes with the naked eye you'd never go to bed.

To keep the dust mite population under control in your home, you'll need to clean.

Vacuum regularly to remove dust mite food – your skin flakes.

Dust with damp cloths to avoid making dust airborne.

Air your house and bed daily.

Launder your sheets once a week in a 60°C wash. Wash your duvet and pillows regularly.

Turn your mattress periodically and replace at the end of the guarantee.

Flies

These really are drawn to filth offenders. They love living in a tip. They're not fussy where or what they land in before touching down on your food.

They have to liquefy solid food with their saliva before they can eat it.

Flies spread bacteria which cause diarrhoea, dysentery, typhoid and cholera. It has been calculated they carry up to 2 million bacteria on their bodies.

Flies are fast breeders. Females lay several batches of 150 eggs at a time. The eggs hatch in 24 hours, and larvae feed on rotting organic matter.

Flies don't like clean homes.

Deny them access to food – don't leave scraps out anywhere.

Don't allow access to rotting fruit or vegetables.

Don't leave defrosting food uncovered.

Use kitchen bins with tight-fitting lids – flies like to lay their eggs in rubbish.

Wipe down surfaces with clean cloths before food preparation.

Rodents (rats and mice)

Rodents play host to parasites that spread diseases such as salmonella, meningitis, encephalitis and tapeworms. In the 14th century rats spread bubonic plague, killing half the population of Europe.

Mice will eat anything and can survive on the smallest scraps of food.

Mice are incontinent, they urinate constantly and produce around 80 droppings a day. Rats' urine contains micro-organisms that cause serious illness in humans.

Mice breed very quickly. One pair and their progeny can produce 200 offspring a year. Rodents are best controlled by good housekeeping.

Non-refrigerated food should be stored in closed jars or sealed plastic storage bins. Scraps of food dropped on floors and surfaces must be cleaned up.

Pet food bowls should be emptied and cleaned after eating.

Rodent infestations are hard to shift and require professional help.

getting started

getting started

Fleas and bed bugs

These pests bite! They have piercing, sucking mouthparts. They can cause medical problems – flea allergy, tapeworms and anaemia.

Fleas are excellent jumpers, leaping up to 20 cm vertically and 30 cm horizontally.

Normally after a blood meal the female flea can lay 20 eggs, which hatch in two days.

Vacuum regularly – this removes eggs and fleas. Put a pet flea collar in the vacuum cleaner bag, and change the bag regularly.

Treat pets, and the home if necessary, with regulatory products that stop flea larvae becoming adults.

Avoid using secondhand bedding and mattresses which may contain bed bugs. Secondhand furniture may also harbour fleas and bugs.

Pantry pests

These are mainly beetles that live on stored foods with low moisture content, such as flour, biscuits, cereals, nuts, dried pasta.

They lay their eggs in the food. When the larvae hatch they tunnel through the food, build a cocoon and pupate. They can penetrate paper, cardboard and cellophane packaging.

Never leave open packets in your cupboards. Keep foods in airtight glass, metal or heavy plastic containers. Use older batches of food first. Don't buy more food than you can reasonably use.

Vacuum the corners of cupboards to remove insect eggs and webbing, then wipe and dry. Check drawers where you keep baking utensils.

Textile pests

There are two main types: carpet beetles and clothes moths. Females lay up to 100 eggs, which can hatch in eight days.

If you have a problem with these it will usually indicate a dirty home.

Textile pests feed on animal fibres like wool, fur, feathers and silk.

It's the larvae that do the munching. They like their textiles dirty, they need the grime, sweat and urine too. They leave a trail of destruction as they munch through carpets, clothes, rugs and upholstery.

Regular vacuuming and laundering are the best weapons – removing their food, e.g. hair, lint and crumbs, as well as larvae and eggs.

Steam-cleaning carpets and rugs will help kill carpet beetle larvae.

Don't leave dirty clothes to fester in cupboards. Launder first.

When storing clothes ensure they are freshly laundered and pack with moth balls or cinnamon sticks and cloves to deter moths.

getting started

Now you've discovered just what you can end up sharing your home with, it's time to start cleaning!

How clean is your routine?

Until well past the middle of the last century housework was a daily routine that dictated what jobs were done on each day of the week. Monday was washday, and women would all race to get their washing on to the line. Chimneys were still in use then, and washing left to dry outside would often become soiled with coal smuts and would have to be done again. Ironing would be done on Tuesday, and during the evening clothes would be mended and socks darned.

On the other days women would clean. Every day the front step would be scrubbed and the water sloshed across the pavement to keep the dirt from coming in. Your neighbours expected all the water to be 'joined up', otherwise they would gossip about your slovenly ways. Shopping would be reserved for the day the wages were brought home in a brown waxy envelope, usually Friday or Saturday. Baking would be done on Saturday, and Sunday was a day of rest, although there would usually be a roast dinner to prepare and cook.

Spring-cleaning was necessary because people heated their homes with open coal fires, lit them with gas lamps and burned candles. The soot and dust had to be cleaned away once the days lengthened, the fires went out and the sun showed up the dirt. For many people this routine continued until at least the 1960s.

Homes lacked the marvellous gadgets we have today. A whistling kettle was considered a great novelty! Carpets were brushed or beaten, driving up clouds of dust. Laundry was done in the sink, and put through the mangle to squeeze out the water. Dishes were always washed by hand, and in the days before fridges and freezers shopping was a far more frequent chore.

When you consider how time-consuming running a home was in the last century, you really have no excuse not to be able to keep up now, even though both men and women tend to go out to work. Haven't things changed! There are many labour-saving devices our predecessors would have given their right arm for. We have vacuum cleaners, washing machines, tumble dryers, dishwashers, enormous fridges and freezers, microwaves, duvets (rarely sheets and blankets), and a dazzling array of products designed to tackle every task.

A tidy home is a clean home

Cleaning will always be easier if you are tidy and put things back each time they are used. Become a gatherer! Pick things up as you go, returning them to their proper place. Keep a little basket by the stairs – don't make unnecessary trips. Get into the habit of scooping things up before bedtime, collecting mugs, glasses, ashtrays, papers and post; give the cushions a bang and everything will be shipshape for the morning. Who wants to be confronted at the start of a new day with yesterday's filth?

We're all hoarders to some degree. If your cupboards and drawers are so crammed full that you are short of storage space and cannot find a permanent home for things, then you need to clear out and dispose of the items you no longer need or use. Your home will be much more comfortable and run more efficiently if things are put away. You will also have the added advantage of being able to locate what you need quickly, without the frustration of searching through endless piles of things. Once clutter is removed you can keep the surfaces clean and healthy.

No, we're not kidding

Do a little bit each day

Some people cannot relax until every last chore is done; others just can't seem to get started, or don't know where to start. We're making a lot of excuses for ourselves about why we don't have time around the home.

Tidy as you go: a quick flick here and there with a duster – don't let it build up, dear – you make life easy or you make life hard, and we know which we prefer. Keep on top of the laundry, restore order in the kitchen after every meal, a quick run round the centre of each room with the vacuum, and you'll be keeping a lovely happy home. If others don't or won't help, don't scream and give yourself a headache – if they want to wallow in their own dirt, let them get on with it!

Get on with it and no moaning, you lazy beggars!

getting started

DAILY ROUTINES

If you try to do the following little tasks every day they will soon become second nature, and you won't even notice you're doing them. A couple of minutes here, a few seconds there, and you'll soon wonder what all the fuss was about.

1 Pull back the bedcovers to air while you shower and breakfast. Open the window: this will reduce humidity and limit the number of dust mites.

2 Keep the kitchen clean and tidy. Wash up after each meal, and keep surfaces clean.

3 Change dishcloths and tea towels daily.

4 Vacuum or sweep the kitchen floor.

5 Keep sinks clean and hand towels fresh.

6 Keep toilets scrupulously clean.

7 Return things to their place so clutter doesn't build up.

8 Consider nominating days for laundry: e.g. Saturday for bedlinen, Monday for towels, Tuesday for coloureds, Thursday for whites. Hang laundry up to dry to make ironing easier.

WEEKLY ROUTINES

Of course there are some jobs you don't need to do every day.
That doesn't mean you have to save them all up for a mammoth
cleaning blitz at the end of the week. Oh please, get a system or
you'll be in one heck of a mess. Do a couple of these things along
with your daily routine and you'll never spend a whole day
cleaning again.

1 Change the bedlinen (twice weekly is best in hot weather).

2 Change bath and shower towels two or three times weekly

3 Vacuum carpets and floors.

4 Wash or mop all hard floors.

5 Dust the surfaces (if you're pressed for time, dusting will always wait – dust doesn't smell but toilets always do).

6 Wipe fingerprints from door handles and light switches (do this as you go round, it only takes a second and keeps germs away).

7 Thoroughly clean the bathroom: toilet, sink, shower, tiles, toothbrush holders, mirrors and floor.

8 Attend to the areas of the kitchen not covered by daily routines: wipe cupboard doors, splashbacks, oven, microwave, fridge, windows, and rinse and disinfect rubbish bins.

9 Iron the laundry.

getting started

MONTHLY ROUTINES

Now don't go thinking we've gone all obsessive here, dear. This isn't about getting down the calendar and marking off great lists of tasks on the first of each month. These are just the little extra things. It would be daft to do them every day or week, why waste your time? But every now and again your home will be cleaner if you tick off some of these extra things. Do you know what I do? I love watching television, but some nights I have a look and I think, 'Well, there's nothing on.' So I think to myself, 'I'll just go and clean a room I haven't done for a while.' Try it – come the end of the evening you feel so good that you haven't wasted your time watching a load of rubbish – and you've got a lovely clean room.

1 Clean windows, inside and out.

2 Launder under bedding, mattress covers and pillow protectors.

3 Turn mattresses (at least every other month).

4 Sort through cupboards and drawers regularly, discarding things you don't use.

5 Vacuum areas you normally neglect – under the bed, curtains, cobwebs in high corners.

6 Clean lamps and lampshades.

7 Polish wooden furniture.

8 Polish mirrors, including frames.

9 Wax floors after washing them.

10 Thoroughly clean inside the oven.

11 Dust blinds, door tops and picture rails.

SPRING-CLEANING (AND AUTUMN-CLEANING)

You know, it sounds old-fashioned, but many people still spring-clean. In the old days they used to wash everything – yes, everything. Empty all the drawers and cupboards, pull out all the furniture, take down all the curtains, wash all the floors and rugs, and scrub down the paintwork. Perhaps people today don't go to quite these lengths, but as the days lengthen, the windows get opened and the sun streams in we start to see the dust and dirt that has been hidden all winter. So give your home a treat. If a home is clean, slavery is over!

1 Wash blankets, duvets and pillows.

2 Change seasonal clothing in wardrobes and pack away clothes not in use.

3 Items you have not worn for over two years should be parted with.

4 Clean the walls, ceilings and floors.

5 Vacuum books, CDs, videos and shelves.

6 Clean underneath heavy furniture and electrical appliances.

7 Shampoo carpets and upholstery

8 Launder or dry-clean curtains and bedcovers.

9 Discard items or appliances that are broken or no longer in use.

10 Inspect garages, basements, lofts and sheds. Spring is a marvellous time to freshen up these areas for the summer – after all, that's where the junk tends to get left, now isn't it?

DEEP-CLEANING – IF YOU ARE STARTING FROM SCRATCH

If you do it little and often your home will never get out of control. However, there are times when you may find yourself inheriting someone else's dirt. You might move into rented accommodation, or buy a new home where the cleanliness leaves a lot to be desired. You might need to help an elderly or unwell relative restore order when through no fault of their own things have slipped out of control. Here is an action plan to launch an assault on the scale we needed for *How Clean Is Your House?*

1 Start at the top of the house and work down.

2 Clean top to bottom of every room.

3 Bedrooms, studies, and reception rooms first.

4 Ceilings, walls, curtains, floors. Pull out all furniture and appliances and clean behind and underneath.

5 Wet first – washing paintwork, windows, laundering, shampooing.

6 Dry next – dusting, polishing, waxing.

7 Vacuuming last – removing all traces of dust and debris.

8 These rooms last – bathrooms, kitchens and utility rooms. As you clean through the home you will be replenishing your buckets, cloths, dusters and mops as you remove the dirt from elsewhere, so save these rooms until last.

9 Finally – attack the porch, hallway, garage, cellar, loft.

Treat yourself, dear!

When all the cleaning is done I like nothing better than to sit down with a long cool glass of sparkling water. You're usually pretty warm, so it's nice to have that cold drink. I find it very refreshing. Then I think to myself, well, that's all done, I'll have a bit of time off now. I'll sit and rub my kitty, Daisy's tummy and she's very happy, and so am I.

kitchen

The kitchen is the engine-room of every household, so make sure it is serviced regularly. For most of us it's where we cook, eat, store our food, deal with our rubbish, and often it's where we do our laundry. In many homes the kitchen also provides another exit, leading out to the garden, from where dirt can easily be tramped back indoors.

We saw some truly terrible kitchens when we were travelling round cleaning up Britain. Filthy, sticky rubbish bins spewed their contents on to the floor, torn black bags sat next to radiators incubating germs, allowing flies to lay their eggs in their favourite haunt. Cupboards were crammed with decaying foods long past their best-before dates, pantry-pest biscuit beetles had moved in to devour leaking packages of pasta, flour and nuts. Grease lined every surface and grill pans swam in slimy debris, occasionally peppered with mouse droppings. Ovens were caked with blackened residue, fridges were awash with age-old spillages, shelves were sticky, drawers were packed with rotting vegetables. Washing up lined every surface, caked in furry green mould-encrusted food residue. The sink was piled high, household cats often licking dirty plates. Dishcloths were sour, scrunched up and stiff, infested with millions of bacteria. Laundry was strewn over tables, even pants and socks – none of them escaped our sniff test! And oh, the honk!

Of course your kitchen needn't look like that and most of them don't (we hope). If you follow our clean-up routine and tips, your kitchen will be a hygienic sanctuary from the world where you can enjoy preparing meals, safe in the knowledge that you won't be poisoning either yourself or anyone else next time you cook.

minging, honking, bogging

Top tips for a clean and safe kitchen

The kitchen can be a very hazardous area, one where a multitude of sins can easily happen. There's a lot going on in here, with cooking, eating and laundry. The kitchen is the heart of the home, so don't give it a coronary!

Remove unnecessary clutter from surfaces. Discard or store appliances and gadgets you don't use any more.

Follow food storage tips.

Keep your fridge clean and tidy. Before you do your weekly shop remove the contents, discarding old food and cleaning shelves and racks.

Wipe your hob each time you use it. Wipe down the surfaces of the oven after each use. It will be much easier to keep it clean that way.

Wipe up spillages in your microwave whenever they occur.

Use a bin with a lid to keep smells at bay and flies out. Empty it as soon as it smells, even if it's not full. Wash and disinfect once a week.

Wipe surfaces down before and after preparing food.

Change the dishcloth you wipe surfaces with every day.

Use two chopping boards, one for raw meat, a separate one for vegetables.

Don't leave dirty crockery and pans to fester where they can attract harmful bacteria.

Keep sink and drainer clean and tidy.

Keep kitchen floors free from debris and grease by sweeping and washing regularly.

If you have pets, don't leave their dirty food dishes out after meals as they will attract flies and, potentially, rodents.

Cat-litter trays should not be kept in the kitchen. If possible a bathroom, hall or lobby is a better spot.

Don't leave damp or dirty laundry festering in the washing machine or drier, and avoid sorting dirty laundry on food preparation surfaces.

kitchen

Food storage

Don't buy too much food – why buy food you can't eat? It's not cheap, you know. Don't over-stock on fruit and vegetables either, they will rapidly ripen and attract flies. Flies love to lay their eggs in rotting vegetables and fruit, so keep a regular eye on your vegetable rack and fruit bowl too. Be fastidious in your cupboards – you've got eyes, you know when your cupboards are dirty, dear. You don't want larder beetles and moths moving in to devour your food. Keeping dried foods in those super stackable heavy plastic containers is a wonderful way of keeping them out. Here are some handy tips to avoid sharing your meals with a whole host of unwanted guests.

You know when your cupboards are dirty, dear!

STAR TIP
To make your kitchen smell divine, fill a small saucepan with water and bring to a simmer. Then add cinnamon, cloves, vanilla and orange peel.

Don't allow fruit kept in bowls to become over-ripe. It will attract fruit flies.

Keep an eye on your vegetables. Discard rotten ones, as they will cause others to rot quickly too.

Check the contents of the fridge every couple of days. You're always popping in for the milk, so have a nose round. Discard foods that are past their best.

Keep raw meats on the bottom shelf so that they can't drip and contaminate foods below.

Cooked meats should always be stored above raw meats.

Know your cupboards. Go through food cupboards every couple of months, wiping the shelves and discarding food that has passed its best-before date. Dry the shelves thoroughly before bringing older stocks to the front, putting newer to the back.

Keep flour, nuts, biscuits, rice, pasta and other dried foods in tightly sealed glass or heavy plastic containers to stop pantry-pest beetles and moths getting inside.

Don't leave foodstuffs out on work surfaces after preparing meals.

Let the white show!

The kitchen takes a mighty hammering, doesn't it, what with all the condensation and grease generated every time you cook. You make life easy, or you make life hard, so don't stop at the dirt you can see, have a regular set-to.

Fill a bowl with hot soapy water, and don't tickle, dear, scrub! Start with the cupboards, inside and out. Wipe down the doors, the drawers and the handles too. Leave it all crisp and smashing, it's so lovely to see the white. No matter how careful you are, things will always get underneath, so have a good scrub. Every scrap of food is a feast for bacteria, a reservoir for germs and an attraction for pests. And we don't want to give them a chance, do we now?

Surfaces

Keep all surfaces spotlessly clean. Wipe down behind any surface appliances such as kettles, toasters, coffee-makers, food processors and microwaves, and of course clean the appliances themselves. Use hot soapy water and a clean cloth – otherwise you'll just be spreading bacteria round. Don't neglect splashbacks, handles or light switches – anything you touch while you are preparing food.

HOW TO CLEAN KITCHEN SURFACES

Remove loose food remains by scooping crumbs up into your hand with a damp cloth or paper towel.

Avoid sweeping debris on to the floor.

Have a bit of rough! A cotton-weave dishcloth (not the one you use for the dishes) is best for wiping with hot soapy water. The texture of the cloth helps remove residue. These dishcloths are so tough you can even boil them clean.

There's no need to use anti-bacterial cleaners all the time – hot soapy water is very effective.

Air dry or wipe dry with a fresh cloth or paper towel. You probably want to get everything back in place quickly, so why not dry? It only takes a moment.

Washing up

Even if you have a dishwasher you'll want to wash the odd thing by hand. Why run a whole machine for a couple of breakfast bowls and mugs?

Isn't it funny how the washing up is such a source of argument? People get along just fine until a few pots need washing and then there are cross words, and fights break out starting with lines like, 'I did the cooking,' or, 'I did it last time.' One dirty mug left unwashed on the drainer soon becomes a small army, and the next thing you know it's a washing-up nightmare.

GRIME FILE
It's best to wash all dirty dishes in hot soapy water as soon as possible. If you're busy entertaining, at least rinse the dishes under the hot tap. When you let dirty dishes sit for a long time the food contributes nutrients for bacteria, so they will rapidly multiply.

Hot soapy suds

HOW TO WASH UP

Start with a nice clean sink. Wash out the bowl and wipe down the drainer with hot soapy water. Don't stand your clean dishes in dirt – they will pick up bacteria.

We like to use a plastic bowl. It requires less water to fill than a sink. It also cushions the dishes.

Run hot water with a squirt of concentrated washing-up liquid. You'll need less water with a bowl, so you'll have plenty of hot left for rinsing.

Rubber gloves will protect your hands, and allow you to use slightly hotter water.

Use a nylon brush and a cotton cloth. Soapy wire pads are good for some pans, but never use on non-stick ones.

Scrape the plates.

Place the washing up in piles corresponding with the order in which it will be washed. For goodness sake don't stretch over piles of pans to reach the glasses.

After washing each item, rinse it in clean hot water. Use a second bowl, or run under the hot tap.

Change the water regularly.

Dry dishes with a cloth, and have plenty of clean ones to hand.

WHAT IS THE CORRECT
ORDER FOR WASHING UP?

Glasses – always do special glass that you treasure separately. Either put it to one side and do it last, using fresh water, or do it first and put it away safely.

Lightly soiled dishes – saucers, jugs, side plates.

Cups and mugs.

Plates (food remains scraped and rinsed off).

Cutlery.

Cooking dishes and pans.

STAR TIP
Get rid of garlic smells on your hands by rubbing them on the metal tap.

DIRTY CLOTHS SPREAD GERMS

Don't use one cloth for everything. Keep two separate cloths, one for dishes, one for wiping down surfaces.

Don't store them near food or on clean surfaces.

Never wipe your hands on tea towels – you will transfer germs from your hands. Use a separate hand towel, or paper towels.

Use cotton dishcloths. Their waffle weave provides slight abrasion, helping to remove dirt, and they last longer when washed.

After washing up, leave the cloths to soak in a solution of washing-up liquid with a couple of drops of bleach added.

Wash dishcloths and tea towels daily in a hot wash (60°C).

You can even pop dishcloths into the dishwasher each time you do a load.

Replace with new cloths on a regular basis.

To clean up raw meat juices and spillages it is best to use paper towels and discard.

GRIME FILE
Within eight hours one bacterium can multiply to 16 million on a damp dirty cloth. Surfaces are more often contaminated after they've been cleaned, by wiping with unclean cloths. Around 79 per cent of people change their dishcloths less than once a month and 87 per cent rinse the dishcloth in dirty washing-up water.

Sponges
are slovenly

Ooh, what the eye can't see in all those little holes! Bacteria wandering in, who knows what they're up to in there out of sight? It's like a Swiss cheese in those sponges. You can see where you are with a cloth, dear. A nice fresh waffle-weave cotton cloth is the tool of a true cleaning queen!

Chopping boards

Always use two chopping boards, one for raw meat, a separate one for vegetables.

Germs can survive on chopping boards for several hours. Always scrub chopping boards with hot soapy water and rinse under hot running water.

Dry with paper towel to avoid cross-contamination with germs on cloths.

To remove strong odours such as onion and garlic, squeeze lemon juice onto the board and wipe with a damp cloth.

HANDY TIPS FOR REMOVING FOOD STAINS FROM COOKING UTENSILS

Baking trays and roasting tins – add a cup of biological washing powder to warm water and soak. You can remove tougher stains by heating gently on the hob for 10 minutes.

Boil tartare sauce in water to remove the 'rainbow' effect from aluminium pans.

Clean rust from knives by leaving the blade stuck in a raw onion. Wiggle it around to activate the juice.

To remove tea stains from mugs and cups, rub with a paper towel and a little salt, borax or bicarbonate of soda. The mild abrasive action removes the mark wonderfully.

For heavily stained mugs, fill with water and a little bleach and leave to stand for 5 minutes, but you'll have a lot of rinsing to do.

Pans are easier to clean if you soak them immediately in cold water with a drop of washing-up liquid.

To remove rust from cast-iron pans and woks, rub with the cut side of half a potato dipped in concentrated washing-up liquid. Rinse, then wipe with cooking oil and paper towel.

To remove the tarnish from copper cookware, sprinkle with salt, cover with lemon juice or vinegar, then rub the affected area again. Rinse thoroughly and buff dry.

A dash of distilled white vinegar in the final rinse will bring a lovely sparkle to glassware.

Remove red wine stains from the bottom of a decanter by adding a few grains of rice and some distilled white vinegar. Rotate gently, the abrasive action of the rice will gently remove inaccessible deposits.

kitchen

How clean is your cooker?

If you spotted a dirty oven or hob in your local takeaway you would be horrified, yet many people are happy to dish up meals from dirty cookers in their own home. Old, decaying food remains equal germs, so make sure you clean your hob after each use, and mop up spills in your oven as they occur – it will be easier to clean.

The hob

Hot soapy water and a clean dishcloth are usually sufficient.

Ceramic and halogen hobs should be cleaned with the product recommended by the manufacturer. Wipe up sticky spills immediately or sugar can crystallize and cause the hob to become damaged. Use a specialist hob scraper to remove burnt-on residue.

Gas rings should be dismantled and cleaned in hot soapy water with a nylon pad.

Oven

Always follow the manufacturer's instructions, particularly for self-cleaning panels.

In an ideal world, wipe inside the oven after each use. For stubborn marks or dirty ovens you will need a full-strength oven cleaner. These can be very toxic. Wearing a face-mask, goggles and long rubber gloves may seem extreme, but such attire is necessary to prevent accidents. Cover the floor with newspaper to stop spillages damaging the surface.

STAR TIP
To help keep the oven clean, lay a sheet of aluminium foil in the bottom and simply discard when dirty. But don't neglect your shelves, dear; don't let dirt build up, for goodness' sake.

Grill pan

Grill pans should be washed after every use. Line them with aluminium foil and simply remove the foil after use – it's a lot less bother than scrubbing.

Accumulated fat can cause fires.

Don't pour the grease down the sink, it can cause blockages. Allow to cool, then wipe away with paper towels and scoop into a bin-bag.

Use hot soapy water. You can even put the grill pan in the dishwasher.

Cooker hood and filter

Don't forget to wipe dust and grease from the cooker hood with hot soapy water.

The metal filter should be removed from time to time and scrubbed with hot soapy water and a nylon brush. Some are designed to go in the dishwasher.

Charcoal and paper filters need to be replaced regularly: charcoal every three months, paper every two.

STAR TIP
Stainless steel cooker hoods can be kept shiny and streak-free by using a spray lubricant and wiping over with paper towels, which will also make cleaning easier. Baby oil has a similar effect.

kitchen

How clean is your microwave oven?

We've seen some truly disgusting microwaves on our travels. Burned-on food stains, ovens thick with grease, the glass so dirty you could barely see in, and the smell of old curry. Urgh! Microwaves are designed to be quick and simple to use, and guess what? They are also quick and easy to clean!

1 Wipe over with a damp cloth soaked in hot soapy water after each use.

2 Remove and wash the glass turntable in hot soapy water or pop it into the dishwasher.

3 Vacuum the vents with the soft brush attachment.

4 To remove stains from white interiors, use a paste of bicarbonate of soda and water. Don't use steel wool pads as they could scratch and lead to rusting.

STAR TIP
To loosen dirt and grease inside the microwave, put a few slices of lemon in an uncovered bowl of water and cook on high for 3 minutes. The condensation from the steam will loosen the dirt, the lemon will freshen the oven and deodorize lingering smells.

kitchen

How clean is your fridge?

You're always popping in and out of the fridge for the milk, so get into the habit of having a good look round. If you see something that's past it, for heaven's sake throw it out, don't keep it lingering around. Any spills, mop them up right away, don't give the germs a chance. You're keeping your food in a fridge for a reason, dear, to keep it safe, so why be all unsavoury inside?

Many modern fridges are frost-free and don't need defrosting. However, if you have an ice-making compartment is it important to keep this clear of ice so that frozen foods can be kept safely, and so that the door closes snugly. Despite the need for less defrosting, the fridge should still be washed frequently.

Once a week, before you go shopping, pull everything out and have a good sort through. It's a jolly good way of reminding yourself what you need to buy, too. Heavens, the times we've come back from the shops without things – isn't it annoying? Pull out the shelves and the drawers and give them a little wash over with warm soapy water, and put back all the contents in a nice neat order. Don't forget, when you bring the lovely fresh food home, to put it behind the older foods which you really must use up first. Who wants to waste good food?

Finally, do check your temperature, dear. It should be at 4°C please, and don't cram your fridge with unnecessary stuff – let the air circulate.

STAR TIP
Clean out your fridge before you go shopping. You'll have a nice clean home for fresh food when you get back, and you'll discover what you are running out of before you get to the shops, not when you get home.

CLEANING THE FRIDGE

First, turn the fridge off.

Cleaning is easiest when food stocks are low. Remove all the food, putting perishable foods into a cool bag or box if you have one.

Remove the shelves and drawers.

Wash these in warm soapy water (washing up liquid works well, but avoid strong fragrances), rinse well and allow to air dry.

You can use a solution of bicarbonate of soda if you don't want to use detergent.

Wash the interior walls, top and bottom and the door panel.

Wipe or gently brush the door seals with a damp cloth or toothbrush.

Periodically pull out the fridge. Wipe down the sides you don't normally see and vacuum the condenser coil on the back with the soft brush attachment. Removing the dust will allow the coils to work more efficiently. Don't forget to clean the floor underneath while you're at it.

Seal strong-smelling foods in plastic containers to prevent unpleasant odours.

kitchen

STAR TIP
Fill a clean sock or nylon stocking with freshly ground coffee and pop inside the fridge to help deodorize any smells.

How clean is your freezer?

There's really no need to clean the freezer every week, thank goodness – why give yourself a hard life? However, unless you have a modern frost-free model you will still have to defrost it from time to time. The more frequently you open the door, the more frequently you will need to defrost it. That's because the water vapour in the air that gets into the freezer every time you open the door will form ice once it freezes.

Finally, dear, the correct temperature for the freezer to run at is -18°C.

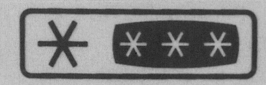

STAR TIP
You can help prevent your freezer from icing up quickly by opening the door less often and for a shorter time. The super-organized keep a list of the food that's inside, instead of opening the door and rummaging through the shelves each time.

CLEANING THE FREEZER

1 This is best done when your food stocks are running low and in cooler weather.

2 Go through the food, chucking out things that are past their best or that you don't plan to use. Don't let your freezer be a holding station for the bin!

3 Put the food you are keeping into a cool bag or box.

4 Stand bowls of very hot water on tea towels on the shelves to steam off the ice more quickly. Catch the drips in a bowl on the bottom.

5 Change the bowls of hot water as they cool.

6 Don't scrape at the ice with anything sharp, you may damage the cooling coils. If you must scrape, use a rubber spatula.

7 While the freezer defrosts, wash the drawers with warm soapy water and leave to air dry.

8 Once the ice has melted, wipe down the inside and the door panel just as you do the fridge, with warm soapy water.

9 If your freezer has a drip pan at the back, clean this too.

10 Vacuum the external cooling coils at the rear of the freezer, using a soft brush attachment, to remove the dust and keep the freezer working more efficiently.

STAR TIP
If you don't have a cool bag or box, put the frozen food into a black plastic sack, and then wrap this in a duvet to insulate the contents while you get to work.

kitchen

How clean is your kitchen sink?

Who doesn't like a nice shiny sink? We're all so proud of our new kitchens these days, aren't we? The sink is a vital part of your kitchen equipment. It's used for preparing vegetables, meat, fish and other food, and washing up dishes and pans you plan to eat from, so keep it clean. Those who are fastidious about hygiene don't even use their sink for washing dirty hands, let alone cleaning shoes or washing out paintbrushes! Even we wouldn't go that far, but there's no accounting for some. Don't be mucky with your sink, as bacteria could soon infect your food and then upset tummies or even worse are likely to follow.

What aren't kitchen sinks made of these days? Goodness, there's such a choice: stainless steel, ceramic, acrylic, to name just a few. Always follow the manufacturer's instructions when cleaning the surfaces; whatever they are made from, it is important to keep them spotless.

Please don't be lazy about taps. A little wipe round with the cloth, buffing dry, brings them up looking lovely and takes away all those nasty water spots. Give the drain and overflow a bit of attention too – a bottle-brush is wonderful for reaching inside.

CLEANING THE KITCHEN SINK

Lemon juice is a natural corrosive that can be used to remove limescale deposits from chrome kitchen taps (but not plated taps). Rub half a lemon over the surface, leave for a few minutes and then rinse thoroughly. For heavily scaled taps, repeat as necessary.

Distilled white vinegar is also excellent for removing limescale from chrome and stainless steel. Rub on with paper towels, leave for a few hours, then rinse thoroughly. This also removes water marks from stainless steel sinks and drainers. Wipe dry with paper towels.

To remove rust marks from stainless steel sinks, rub with a little lighter fluid.

Ceramic sinks get discoloured easily. To restore whiteness, fill the sink with cold water, add a cupful of bleach and leave to soak.

Don't neglect plugholes and overflows. Use a bottle-brush to scrub inside.

STAR TIP
Keep drains running freely by once a month running through a handful of washing soda crystals followed by a kettle full of boiling water.

Washing machine

Gosh, we're jolly lucky to have these. Time was when washday really meant all day, but pop the laundry in now and it's over in a trice. There really is no excuse for piles of washing everywhere, especially now we've got dryers too. We don't know we're born sometimes. Treat your machine with kindness and it really will pay dividends.

Keep the drain filter clean – the machine will work better and you will avoid it flooding. It's amazing how much fluff collects, not to mention stray buttons and coins.

Pull out the detergent drawer and rinse out deposits of powder and fabric conditioner. This also prevents flooding.

Wipe the door seal with a soft, damp cloth or an old toothbrush to remove soap scum.

Every now and again run the machine empty, without detergent, to give it a good rinse. A proprietary limescale remover run through with the machine empty will help the heating element last longer, stopping it from furring up with limescale (just as kettles tend to).

kitchen

Dishwasher

These really are marvellous inventions. But they don't look after themselves, you know. A little attention now and again and they will repay you with fresh-smelling and sparkling glasses and dishes time after time.

1 Run a cup of white vinegar through the entire cycle of the dishwasher when empty. It will remove all the grease and soap scum and leave it sparkling clean and fresh.

2 Remove the filter regularly and clean with hot soapy water.

3 Keep the water-spray arms free of limescale. Use a needle to poke out any hard deposits.

4 For sparkling clean dishes and a lovely fragrance, run the washing-up cycle with half a lemon on the top rack. Ooh ... lovely!

Ooh...lovely!

KITCHEN BINS

Oh, we've seen some horrors, we really have. Who wants to live with their own filth for days on end? The kitchen bin really should be emptied every day, sometimes even more often. If you flip the lid and are greeted by a little whiff of a smell, then it really is time for a fresh new bag. And please, dear, never let the bin overflow. Keep the lid clean (paper towel is best), and then once a week wash the whole thing down inside and out. And finally, whatever they say, bins don't last for ever, you know. Treat yourself to a new one every now and again – who wants the same stinky old bin for ten years?

1. The kitchen bin is a bacteria hot spot.

2. Use a bin with a lid.

3. The outside of the bin can easily get contaminated when hands and waste food touch it, so wipe it clean frequently.

4. Use lining bags, don't put rubbish straight into bins.

5. Empty the bin regularly, especially if it starts to smell. Don't wait until it is full (or even overflowing!).

6. Once a week, wash and disinfect the whole bin, inside and out.

Keeping other kitchen equipment clean

Scrub, dear, don't tickle. Do please remember that as sure as eggs is eggs, things will have got underneath your bread bin, your toaster, all manner of debris. It's nice to have some pretty gadgets out on top – if you've got them, why not show them off? But please, not horrible greasy grimy gadgets – keep those shiny surfaces sparkling!

Kettle

To keep your kettle free of limescale, add a solution of water and distilled white vinegar, half and half. Leave to soak and then rinse well.

Coffee maker

Fill the reservoir with undiluted white vinegar. Insert a filter paper as normal, and run half the vinegar through. Leave for 30 minutes and then run the rest through. Rinse twice by flushing through with fresh water.

Toaster

Don't forget to empty the crumbs out every now and again. Simply tip the toaster upside down over the sink or a sheet of newspaper and shake gently. Give the toaster a wipe over with a damp soapy cloth to remove fingerprints and bacteria. If you have a shiny stainless steel model, a little metal polish works wonders.

Food processor

If you keep yours on the work surface, pull it out and clean underneath. Wipe over the appliance and wash the attachments in hot soapy water or pop them in the dishwasher. Use a toothbrush or cocktail stick in the crevices.

Cooking utensils

If you display yours out on top, make sure they stay clean. The tools you use less often will soon collect grease, dust and germs, so pop them in with the washing up from time to time.

STAR TIP
A couple of denture-cleaning tablets added to the water in your kettle and left overnight will also loosen limescale deposits. Simply wipe away in the morning with paper towels. Rinse well before re-use.

Don't be a mucky puppy underfoot. Who wants to drag their feet across a horrible sticky floor? We've seen some horrors, let me tell you. In one house, when we peeled back the lino round the cooker, the floor was alive with slimy grot! It could break your heart, really it could. Even if you can't see them, microscopic scraps of food are bacteria heaven, and germs will happily multiply, undoing all your hard work up top. Spilled crumbs and food will also attract flies and rodents, and who wants them around? You can't get over-familiar with your mop, you know!

Rub-a-dub-dub

HOW TO CLEAN YOUR FLOOR

Whatever the surface, it needs washing regularly. Daily is best; this is an area of heavy foot-traffic.

Sweep up or vacuum all the loose dirt.

Use hot water and detergent.

The two-bucket method works well. Fill one with the cleaning solution and put the wringer on the other. Squeeze the dirty water into the empty bucket.

Use a different mop for the kitchen. Not the one you use for the bathroom.

Always leave your mop to dry head up. If you leave it damp in a bucket bacteria will grow and a nasty pong will soon follow. Ooh, what a honk!

Mops are good but there's no substitute for hands and knees every now and again. Use a wide weave cotton floor cloth and really get in those corners. Scrub dear, don't swish.

living
room

How could anyone survive in the horrible hovels we saw on our travels? And they had the cheek to call them living rooms! Not even the houseplants could manage to breathe. They were slumped in their pots, gasping for air, every leaf carpeted with years of gently descending dust.

A glance around these living rooms revealed a state of terrible human decay and dirt. There were piles of papers, discarded drink cans, empty bottles, half-eaten meals buried under mould, scattered cushions, crumbs underfoot, stains on the carpet, grot on the chairs, grime on the sofas, windows blackened with a thick film of filth. These Aladdin's caves were littered with defunct computers, broken-down tellys, old rolls of carpet, rickety chairs and long-silenced stereos.

living room

These living rooms were crying out to be cleaned. Long-forgotten ornaments begged for attention, hoping to shed their coats of dust and stand proud once again. Television pictures blinked valiantly through filth-fogged screens.

Of course there is no need to let your living room turn into a lair. A well-ordered routine at the end of every day, a couple of jobs once a week, and your living room will become a sanctuary from the world where you can relax and unwind. So let's get cleaning!

De-clutter as you go, dear

If you dump just two things in your living room every day, by the end of the month you will have amassed a vast collection of 60 abandoned articles. Combat this clutter by returning things to their place as you go. At the end of each evening spend a couple of moments gathering up mugs and glasses, returning them to the kitchen; empty bins and ashtrays, collect newspapers and post and put out for recycling, bang your cushions back into shape and pick up bits from your carpet. If someone unexpected visits in the morning you'll never again need to wonder which room to show them into!

How to make dusting easier

Lovely soft furnishings, elaborate curtaining and wall-to-wall carpeting are all huge collectors of dust. While we relax reading, watching television and gossiping we continue to shed skin cells, and you really must pay the same attention to the dust in the living room as you do in the bedroom. The living room tends to have plenty of surfaces that attract dust: tables, lamps, display cabinets, televisions, stereos, entertainment systems, and so on. The less clutter you have on display, the easier it will be to keep dust at bay.

THE BEST WAY TO DUST

When dusting you need to collect it, not disperse it. Use a slightly damp duster that the dust will cling to. Rinse it out in clean water as you go.

Vacuuming furniture and surfaces with a soft brush attachment is most effective when dust has built up. Buff with a dry duster.

Use the vacuum cleaner's soft brush attachment to collect dust from skirting boards and picture rails.

Delicate dusty ornaments are best washed in a bowl of warm soapy water and dried with a tea towel.

Create homes for your possessions. Video tapes, CDs and books will leave your room easier to clean if they are stored away rather than strewn across carpets and surfaces. Cupboards are better than shelves, as you won't spend your life dusting the cases.

Tidy coffee tables at the end of each day, returning books to the shelves, cups to the kitchen and putting newspapers into the recycling box.

Have a few choice ornaments rather than many – they will be easier to keep clean and will look better.

If you do have a large collection, display it behind glass so that you won't be constantly dusting.

Use a desk with a drawer, or create a box file, to store all the paperwork awaiting attention.

Computers tend to attract clutter and dust – consider using a desk unit that is totally enclosed by doors and can be shut.

STAR TIP
Remove dust from plant leaves by stroking them with the soft inside of a banana skin. The dust clings to the skin, and the juice nourishes the leaves.

The home office

If you don't have enough space for a separate office, the living room may often have to serve this function as well. If this is the case, you will have to be extra careful about how much clutter you create. Papers and printers, disks and stationery can rapidly escalate out of control, so consider using a desk that can be totally shut away behind doors. This will keep everything free from dust, which can be especially harmful to computers.

To remove dust and crumbs from computer keyboards, use the soft brush attachment of the vacuum cleaner. You can also use the same attachment over the monitor casing.

To clean the keys, use a cotton bud dipped in warm soapy water and patted dry.

Computer shops sell aerosols with compressed air which will blast out dust and crumbs from keyboards.

Computer screens can be wiped clean with a drop of washing-up liquid on a damp paper towel. Wipe clean with a clean damp paper towel and buff dry.

Aren't you the high-tech one, dear!

How clean are your walls?

Wall-coverings can be delicate, so always test cleaning methods on an inconspicuous area out of sight (behind furniture, for example).

To remove fingermarks from walls, dab firmly with a chunk of white bread.

On painted walls use a mildly abrasive cream cleaner and a soft cloth to remove dirt and marks. Pay special attention to the walls above radiators, where the rising heat attracts dirt.

Remove coloured crayon marks from painted walls by scrubbing with toothpaste. The abrasive action removes the mark.

living room

How clean is your upholstery?

CARING FOR UPHOLSTERY

Vacuum upholstery regularly, at least once a week. Crumbs and other bits rub against the fabric when you sit and gradually wear away the weave and pile.

Bang the cushions and shake the seat pads back into shape at the end of each evening, and the sofa and chairs will repay your effort with years of extra wear. Rotate them from time to time to even out the wear – we all have our favourite seat.

Steam cleaning is another very effective method. You can hire a machine and do it yourself, or call in the professionals. Cleaning will be more successful when done regularly than if left for many years.

Remove spots and stains from upholstery as quickly as possible. Use a proprietary upholstery cleaner; alternatively use shaving foam applied with a clean cloth. Take a dry piece of cloth and bang to avoid leaving watermarks. Dry with a fan or hairdryer.

To remove pet hair from upholstery, take a chamois leather, dampen it, then wring out as tightly as you can. Rub the chamois gently across the fabric and the pet hair will gather neatly in a ribbon as you work over the surface.

To protect the finish of your leather furniture, clean it with real soap products only. Saddle soap is ideal: you can buy it from riding shops and hardware stores.

STAR TIP
To remove chewing-gum from upholstery, place ice cubes in a plastic bag and leave on the gum until brittle, then scrape it off.

LAMPSHADES

1 Lampshades can be dusted with a soft brush, or you can use the soft brush attachment on the vacuum cleaner.

2 Alternatively, remove the shade and roll a barely damp duster over the surface, collecting the dust as you go.

3 Flicking the surface of the lampshade with a damp duster will release the more stubborn dust.

4 Washable fabric lampshades can be cleaned in the bath. Add a little non-biological washing powder, or detergent formulated for woollens, to a bath of warm water, and gently soap the surface of the lampshade with a soft brush. Hang the shade up to drip-dry over the bath by attaching string to the lamp-holder. Finish off with a hairdryer.

5 Don't panic if the braid or trim comes unstuck – a little adhesive will soon re-attach it.

living room

STAR TIP
A sock on a wire coat hanger makes an amusing and practical substitute for a feather duster.

How clean are your windows?

Condensation tends to form on the windows in living rooms, as they are often kept at a higher temperature than other rooms. Windows should be cleaned as and when necessary. You probably won't need to do it every week, but it will be much easier if you give them a quick wipe over frequently.

For super sparkling non-smeary windows, use the vinegar method! Mix one part distilled white vinegar to nine parts water in a spray bottle. Spray sparingly on to the glass and either buff dry with paper towel or, using the traditional method, polish with scrunched-up newspaper. The print on the paper adds to the shine, and it's cheap. However, the print does tend to get on your hands, so feel free to wear rubber gloves.

Wash very dirty windows using a bowl of warm water with a little washing-up liquid. Wipe the soapy water over the windowpane and dry with a clean lint-free cloth or chamois leather.

Break a nail,
it'll break your heart

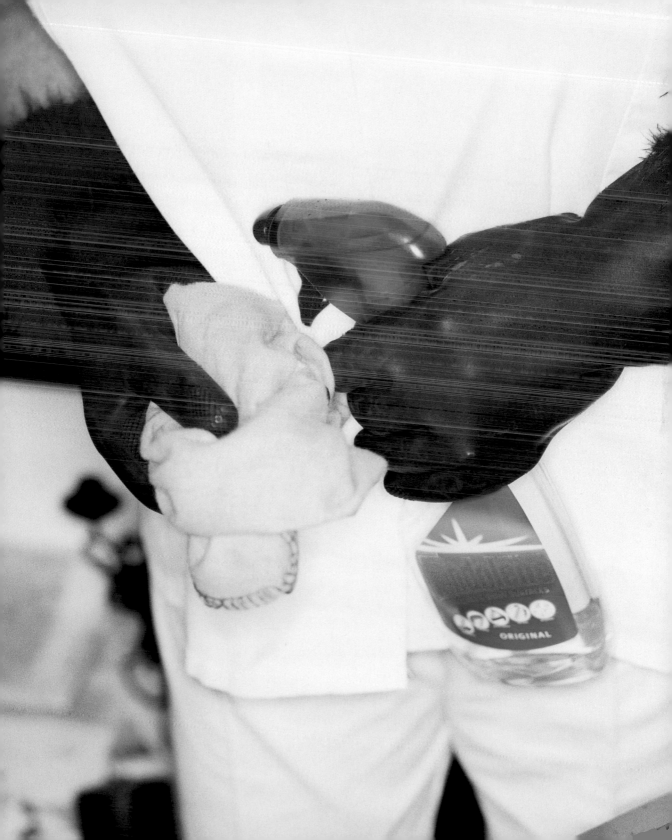

living room

How to remove marks from wooden furniture

The best way to avoid spoiling your wooden furniture with scratches and water marks is to use coasters and mats for glasses, mugs and vases. Choose coasters with a wipeable laminated surface and a layer of felt underneath to give the best protection. Leave them scattered around so that your guests will know to use them. It's often best to consult a furniture specialist when disaster strikes as you may only make the damage worse.

1 Water rings – these don't form in the wax or polish, but in the surface of the wood itself. Always act quickly. For waxed wood, rubbing with a little white spirit will often remove the mark. Other finishes can be trickier.

2 Disguising water marks and rings is another approach. Rub a little cigarette ash into the mark with your finger, and then buff with furniture polish. Alternatively rub a little shoe polish of an appropriate shade into the wood. If the polish shows up too dark, dip a cotton bud in white spirit and rub over the area to dilute the polish to the correct shade.

3 Polish furniture with wax or oil only occasionally. Using a barely damp cloth to collect dust and remove fingermarks is sufficient for weekly cleaning routines. Apply a little furniture polish sparingly and only once a month in order to avoid your furniture becoming polish-bound.

How clean is your fireplace?

Fireplaces are still popular today, even though central heating has largely taken over the main task of heating the home. For a little extra snugness on a cold winter evening there is nothing more comforting than the warm glow of the flames. My, don't surrounds and hearths come in a variety of materials these days? You'll need to keep this area clean when the fire is in use because the soot and debris from the chimney will soon blacken it.

1. Ensure fires are unlit before attempting any kind of cleaning. If the fire is alight you could easily burn yourself, or inadvertently set fire to your clothing.

2. Marble is slightly porous, so be sure to wipe up spillages on hearths and mantels as soon as they occur, and use coasters for drinks and vases.

3. Clean marble by wiping with a mild solution of washing-up liquid and warm water. Buff with a dry cloth.

4. Unvarnished wooden surrounds can be cared for in the same way as wooden furniture. The drying action of the heat means you need to feed the wood with polish more often.

5. Polished slate hearths can be kept shiny and clean with a little oil, rubbed to a shine with paper towel.

6. Metal fire surrounds can be cleaned of soot in a similar way, using spray lubricant and wiping clean with paper towel. The oily film will also make cleaning easier next time.

7. Get your chimney professionally swept from time to time to prevent soot causing a fire.

living room

How clean is your TV?

The static produced by TV sets acts as a magnet, sucking all the dirt from the air towards the screen.

You can use specialist anti-static cleaning cloths to remove this grime, but there are cheaper methods that are just as effective.

A damp paper towel with a drop of concentrated washing-up liquid works well. Buff dry with a clean paper towel.

Use a damp cloth, wrung dry, to wipe the cabinet, ensuring no water enters the grille holes. Dry with a soft cloth.

Use the soft brush attachment of the vacuum cleaner to remove dust from the ventilation grilles at the back of the television set.

Remote controls should also be kept clean. Baby wipes are very useful for this purpose, or cotton buds moistened with warm soapy water. Don't get the keypad wet.

You may well choke –

Be careful about using detergents on the plastic casing, and certainly don't use anything abrasive, which would spoil the finish.

it's your dust!

Absolutely
disgusting

How clean is your carpet?

Many people love the furnished and insulated quality that wall-to-wall carpet gives in the living room – isn't it lovely! However, carpet really is the biggest collector of dust in the whole home – so please, regular vacuuming is a must. If you don't have time to vacuum the whole room, at least do the areas with the most traffic several times a week.

living room

CARE FOR YOUR CARPET

1 Regular and thorough vacuuming is the best way to preserve the appearance and life of your carpet. Pests such as moths, beetles and dust mites are a risk, but regular vacuuming can deter the first two and keep the latter under control.

2 A thorough vacuuming once a week, and partial vacuuming of heavily used areas a couple of times a week, will keep carpets in good condition and dust allergens down.

3 Help protect carpets from heavy furniture and castors by using furniture rests.

4 To remove the indentations caused by heavy furniture on carpets, simply place an ice cube on the spot, allow it to melt, and then tease up the pile gently with a soft brush or cocktail stick.

5 Stains and spills should always be dealt with as quickly as possible. Soak up the residue by blotting, never scrubbing, with a clean white towel or paper towel.

6 For a spill, pour a little soda water over the affected area (half a denture tablet dissolved in water is a good substitute). The bubbles in the water will bring more of the stain to the surface so that it can be blotted away.

7 Once the spill is contained, try to remove any marks using the foam from a little washing-up liquid and water. Use a soft brush, but don't scrub or you will damage the pile.

8 A good way to produce a quantity of foam quickly is to put a finger's width of water in the bottom of a clean empty glass jar and add a few drops of washing-up liquid. Replace the lid and shake vigorously for a few seconds. You will have a jar-full of suds.

9 Blot off the excess foam with a clean white towel. Tread on the towel with both feet to squeeze the excess moisture from the carpet.

To remove tomato ketchup from
carpet, first dab up as much as
possible with paper towels. Spray
the residue sparingly with shaving
foam, wipe away with a damp cloth,
and the ketchup will come away
with the foam.

To remove candle wax from carpet,
lay a thick wad of paper towel or
tissue over the wax and iron with a
warm iron. Press lightly. The wax
will be absorbed into the towel.
(Be very careful not to melt
synthetic carpeting material.)

HOW TO CLEAN YOUR CARPET

If your carpet is subjected to heavy wear, and vacuuming fails to remove all the dirt and marks, it should be shampooed, perhaps as often as every six months. This is especially true if there are allergy sufferers in your household. If you remove your shoes at the door, carpet cleaning may only be necessary every few years or so, depending on how careful you are, and how many people are using your home.

Shampooing – until recent times carpets were shampooed as part of regular spring-cleaning. You can use liquid carpet shampoo, a soft brush, and a vacuum cleaner (designed for this type of usage) for large areas of soiled carpet. This method can tend to over-wet the carpet if you are not careful, and the shampoo can leave a sticky residue which attracts new dirt much more quickly.

Hire a steam cleaning machine. Steam cleaning is a very effective way of cleaning carpets and upholstery, and is the method we used in the television series with our expert cleaner, 'Carpet Dave'. The carpets dry more quickly and more dirt is removed. However, the chemicals can be expensive and the finished result will depend on the quality of the machine and the expertise with which it is used.

Professional carpet cleaners use steam cleaners. Their expertise, combined with the free time you will gain, can be worth paying the extra for. To find a reputable firm, ask for recommendations from a carpet retailer you trust.

Expensive rugs should be professionally cleaned by specialist cleaners. If the rug is worth paying a lot of money for, it is worth the expense of taking it to a professional cleaner who will return it in a thoroughly clean and dry state.

STAR TIP
Keep a bottle of soda water handy for red wine or coffee spills on the carpet. Pour a little over the wet stain, cover with an old clean white towel and press hard to absorb all the moisture. The bubbles help lift the stain.

OOH, WHAT A HONK!
CIGARETTE SMOKE ODOURS

Burning candles will mask the smell of tobacco smoke.

Spray the inside of glass ashtrays with a little of your favourite air-freshener. They will be easier to clean, as the stubs won't stick.

Put a little vanilla essence or lavender oil on to the light bulb when it is switched off. Allow to dry before turning on. When the bulb burns, the vanilla or lavender will emit a pleasant scent.

How clean are your entrance hall, landing and stairs?

We knew that we were in trouble as soon as we crossed the threshold of the homes we had the dubious joy of visiting. First there was the terrible stale stink that rushed out and punched us on the hooter with all the force of a bunch of fives.

Then the grime in the hallway, the filthy paintwork, the grubby fingerprints, the blackened light switches, the cobwebs hanging from every corner and lamp, the carpet with blackened foot-traffic motorways trudged down the middle. Oh, and please, the clutter! Shoes discarded all over the show, rarely in pairs, often in piles. Coats in heaps, or bulging from hooks. Bags abandoned, shopping dumped. Rubbish bags awaiting help off the premises, newspapers collecting in yellowing pyramids. There were bottles for recycling, bicycles leaning, telephone tables groaning, and unwanted post littering all surfaces. Boy, what a welcome!

Furry debris lined every skirting and picture rail, and pictures were hiding behind misted-up glass. Dusty lampshades hung forlornly, bulbs glowing dimly through years of grime. Telephones, slimy with grease, dials and receivers smothered in slime. Ornaments were dulled, marking the passage of time. 'Home sweet home' was never a phrase that sprang to mind. These filth offenders rewrote all the rules: the home as a hovel – oh, the shame.

Make the entrance to your home inviting, a joy to behold, a haven to enter, away from the world. These are the signs of a true cleaning queen's home, so let's get cleaning!

CREATE A GOOD FIRST IMPRESSION

The hallway is the first glimpse your visitors have of your home, so set the right impression from the outset. Have a clean doormat for feet, and a spare hook for coats.

Wash down the paintwork and clean the glass of your front door with warm soapy water. Dry with an old towel or chamois leather.

If you have space, a cupboard for coats and bags will keep things neat and tidy. Keep furniture and clutter to a minimum, as most hallways tend to be long and narrow.

Don't let the hall become a dumping ground: tidy away bags, shopping and newspapers as they arrive. You will probably need a small table for a telephone and mail, and if it has a drawer so much the better.

A well-lit space will help to create a welcoming feel. Try to avoid having a single pendant light fitting, which will create many shadowy corners.

WELCOME

KEEP THE DIRT OUT!

Time was when women washed the step every day, and the water was swilled across the pavement into the gutter to keep the dust and dirt from the street at bay. There was gossip from the neighbours if your water wasn't all joined up with theirs by 10a.m., and cries of 'She isn't even ill, you know!' It's not quite like that today.

1 Plenty of dirt entering the home comes in through the front door. Keep your front path and doorstep swept and clean to prevent dirt and debris from being tramped and blown into your home. Wash the step with warm soapy water

2 Insulate your front door to prevent dust and dirt blowing in around the doorframe.

3 Use a good-quality doormat, which will effectively collect dirt from shoes. Thick coconut-type doormats are good dirt collectors and can be beaten and rolled up into a sausage with bristles outwards to drive out the dirt.

4 If your home has an enclosed outer porch, use a mat there too. Two mats are better than one.

5 Keep slippers by the front door and change into them when you come home. Your carpets will stay cleaner and last longer. Encourage your visitors to remove their shoes when they arrive. Buy some inexpensive slippers for guests to wear, so they feel comfortable.

6 Vacuum the hall and stair carpet or floor-covering at least twice a week, to prevent dirt becoming ground into floors and damaging the pile or scratching the surface.

7 Wash Victorian-style decorative tiled hallways with warm soapy water and dry with an old towel. Cream cleanser will remove stubborn marks. A mix of half water and half distilled white vinegar will restore shine to ceramic tiles. Do not wax the tiles as they will become slippery underfoot – if you wish to seal unglazed tiles, use a proprietary sealant.

halls and stairs

KEEPING WALLS AND PAINTWORK CLEAN

1 Hall and stairway decoration can soon become soiled from fingerprints, scuffmarks from bags and dust from the street. Consider using a durable wall-covering such as washable paint.

2 A dab of cream cleaner is very effective at removing marks from painted surfaces.

3 Wipe skirting boards, dado rails, picture rails and the front doorframe regularly with warm soapy water and a soft cloth. This will prevent dirt building up and spoiling the decor.

THE STAIRS

1 Clutter should never be left on the stairs where it can be tripped over.

2 Vacuum stair carpet at least twice a week to prevent dirt becoming ground into the pile.

3 Wipe banisters and handrails over with a barely damp cloth rinsed with warm soapy water. Buff with a dry cloth.

4 Stairs should be vacuumed from bottom to top to prevent the vacuum cleaner from toppling down the stairs. If the flex isn't long enough to reach the whole flight of stairs, use an extension lead to save having to unplug half-way through the job.

5 Use a crevice nozzle to get into the risers and corners. Use the soft brush attachment to collect dirt and dust from painted areas around the banisters.

STAR TIP
Keep a basket near the bottom of the stairs to collect items that need to be taken upstairs, to avoid having to make unnecessary trips.

CAUTION
Cleaning in
progress

bathroom

Ooh, we witnessed some terrible bathrooms. Some of the loos we peered into were caked with unmentionables, and the honk made us feel sick to our stomachs. Toilet seats covered in urine – why can't men lift the seat and aim straight? They should all be issued with a funnel at birth if they can't train their aim. We don't much like toilet brushes, and after our tour of Britain's filthiest homes we like them even less. Caked in faeces, sitting in holders full of scum, the pathogens lurking really were weapons of mass destruction.

The baths didn't look much better. How were these people keeping themselves clean? The tubs looked as if they had last been used for a mud fight – dirt ingrained all over, with a tidemark higher than Brighton beach. Taps were caked in limescale, and the pong coming out of some of the plugholes made us want to gag. Shower curtains didn't fare much better – mould and mildew spreading like bubonic plague across expanses of putrid plastic.

Toothbrushes sat in mugs of festering scum with mould growing on top, and people were cleaning their teeth with these godforsaken instruments of death. Stare into the bathroom mirror and you could barely see anyone looking back for the filth and dust. Houseplants withered and died on the windowsills, choked under a coat of dust, skin flakes and hair. Towels were damp and mildewed, piled up on the floor, or stiff as a board, draped untidily on a rail and emitting a foul stench that would soon undo any good work done in the bath. The floors were sticky with dried-on pee-pee, and the skirting boards were piled high with insulating layers of hair and fluff.

Why would anyone want to live like this? A clean home is a happy home and cleanliness begins in the bathroom. It only takes a few minutes every day to keep your bathroom shiny, safe and spotless. So let's get cleaning!

bathroom

How clean is your toilet bowl?

Ooh, the toilet. It should be so spotless you could eat your dinner off it, not that you would, of course, but it should be that inviting. Who wants a pongy throne? Of course every home has one – even the Queen goes to the loo, you know, although we expect she has someone to keep it looking nice for her.

Ooh,
what a honk!

Keep your bathroom
smelling fresh by placing
a fabric softener sheet
in the waste basket.

Tips to make your toilet sparkle

For regular cleaning, drop a couple
of denture-cleaning tablets into
the bowl. Leave overnight, but
definitely don't add your false teeth.

Pouring a can of cola into the
bowl and leaving it for an hour
will also remove stains.

Avoid blockages and neutralize
toilet odours by pouring a cup of
bicarbonate of soda into the pan
once a week.

BAN THE BRUSH

Regular viewers will know that we highly disapprove of toilet brushes. Used correctly they're wonderful things but because they are so abused, we say ban the brush. Please retire yours now, and invest in a nice long pair of rubber gloves – your loo will thank you for it, dear.

Toilet brushes are unhygienic because they collect faeces and are often left to sit unwashed in a festering container of bacteria-fuelled water.

Rubber gloves (kept in the bathroom and not used for anything else), paper towel (but don't flush it as it clogs the drain) and lavatory cleaner are the most effective method. Put on those gloves and plunge, dear.

Give the pan a good wipe round, not forgetting under the rim. It's your mess, dear, so don't be too proud.

Wipe round the seat and the area round the hinges. If your hinges are plastic, slip a cleaning wipe between them and the toilet bowl – you'll be amazed at what you find!

If your toilet is caked in filth, try soaking it with limescale remover and then scrub. You can also try baling out the water and covering the limescale with a thick paste of laundry borax and vinegar, leaving it for a couple of hours.

Always leave the toilet pan free of chemicals, as splashing could damage skin.

Don't forget to clean the flush handle with soapy water – people rarely wash their hands before they flush.

Give the seat and lid a nice polish. A squirt of window-cleaning spray works a treat. Job done. That wasn't so bad after all, was it?

IF YOU REALLY MUST BRUSH ...

After use, flush the toilet, add some bleach
and leave the brush to stand in it.

Flush clean water over the brush.

Fill the container with hot soapy water,
then empty the dirty water into the toilet.

Replace the brush regularly.

GRIME FILE

Toilets are regularly
assailed by large quantities
of bacteria. When the user
has a gut infection up to 10
per cent of the bacteria can
be pathogenic, and that's
100 billion bacteria! Vomit
can contain 30 million virus
particles for each millilitre
of liquid. Salmonella has
been shown to survive on
the surface of the toilet for
at least six weeks after an
infection has occurred in the
home. Contact with flushing
handles is a potential hazard,
as most people flush between
using the toilet paper and
washing their hands.

It's filthy,
dirty,

How clean is your bath?

If you're a bubble-bath person you'll know what a pleasure a nice soak is. But who on earth would want to climb into a sticky, grimy bath with a big tidemark round the sides and the flotsam and jetsam of a previous occupant caked on the bottom? I mean, why would they? Now, dear, be considerate, keep the bath sparkling. A quick wipe round with some warm soapy water after every use and you'll never have to scrub again. Keep a cloth handy in the bathroom, and it's done in two minutes. Shiny taps finish the job off nicely – give your taps a treat and dry them off with a towel to stop them spotting with water marks.

stinky

BE A BATHING BEAUTY

Always follow the manufacturer's instructions for cleaning the surface of your bath. Enamel, acrylic and plastic surfaces need different treatment. It's not advisable to use abrasive cleaners on highly polished surfaces.

FIBREGLASS AND ACRYLIC

A mild detergent such as washing-up liquid is best, used with a soft cloth. Dry with a towel to prevent water spots.

If the bath is very dirty, fill it with warm water and biological washing powder. Leave to soak overnight. You can even throw a couple of white shirts in while you're at it.

For a stubborn mark use the mildest abrasive – a paste of baking soda and water. Alternatively try cream of tartar and then rub the surface with half a lemon. Rinse thoroughly.

To remove limescale, try a mixture of half white vinegar and half water. Try to avoid getting the vinegar elsewhere on the bath. Rinse thoroughly, then dry.

ENAMEL

Washing-up liquid is a suitable cleaner, used with a soft cloth. On a dirtier bath use a cream cleaner, but don't over-use or it may eventually dull the surface shine.

Rust stains can be reduced by using lemon juice and salt. Or make a paste of bicarbonate of soda and water, spread over the stain. Leave for one hour, then wipe off. Repeat if necessary.

To remove stubborn limescale marks, take a clean cork from a bottle and use it to rub a little cream cleaner over the affected area. This requires some good old elbow grease, but is very effective.

STAR TIP
If you use your bath as a shower, wash the slip mat on both sides with hot soapy water and a soft brush or cloth. If heavily soiled, soak in the bath with a cup of biological washing powder. If mould has grown on the underside, scrub it away with a nailbrush and a mixture of one part bleach, four parts hot water.

SHOWER CURTAINS

Mould and mildew can be a problem due to the high levels of humidity. Try to use a nylon shower curtain that you can remove easily and put into the washing machine. Ideally have a spare, so you can put the fresh one in place at the same time. Do this frequently to remove soap scum and stop mildew building up.

If you have a heavily soiled non-machine-washable curtain, soak it in a solution of one part bleach to four parts water.

Use an inexpensive washable nylon curtain as a lining inside a novelty curtain.

Machine-wash your shower curtain with a couple of large towels and biological washing powder to remove soap scum. Remove the curtain before the spin cycle, and hang up immediately to let the creases drop out.

Shower curtains can also be washed in a warm bath with a cupful of biological washing powder. After a tiring day, get in and tread it with your bare feet, just like the winemakers do. You'll get a lovely result – and clean feet!

How clean is your shower?

Showering is so quick and easy – just step in and let the water do the work. Cleaning the shower is just as easy, honest, dear. So for heaven's sake don't be silly now, don't let dirt build up: a quick wipe down every day and you'll never have to scrub.

Do you know, some people even wax their bathroom wall tiles with car polish to keep the water marks off? Aren't they the cleaning queens!

Frequent cleaning
makes the job so much easier

1 After you shower, leave the door or curtain open to allow the air to circulate.

2 No more streaky glass. Use a sponge to wipe diluted white vinegar over the door. Buff with a paper towel for sparkling results.

3 Tile grout is porous, and mould and mildew can form due to the high humidity. Mix half bleach and half water and use a toothbrush to clean grout lines between tiles. Work on one line at a time so you can see the result!

4 Tiles are easier to clean if you run the shower on hot for a few minutes to get some steam action going.

5 Soap scum can be removed from tiles with a spray mix of half white vinegar, half water. Rinse and buff dry.

6 A plastic blade window wiper is an excellent tool for swishing the water off shower tiles so that water marks don't form. You can also keep your tiles free of water marks by polishing with car wax!

7 To clean chrome shower heads, remove and immerse in a mix of half white vinegar and half water. Leave for an hour, and repeat as necessary then rinse. (This is not recommended for plated surfaces.)

8 Heavily limescaled plastic and chrome shower heads can be soaked overnight. Douse paper towels in equal parts vinegar and water and attach to the shower head in a plastic bag held in place with an elastic band. Rinse thoroughly and dry.

STAR TIPS
• Showering uses two thirds less water than taking a bath.
• Sharing a shower saves even more water and can be fun with the right companion.
• House plants appreciate a good shower too – leaves the leaves lovely!

How clean is your basin?

A shiny fresh basin is a treat to behold. Do you know what many people say they like about having a cleaner? They come home and their taps are shiny! Honestly, that's it, yet they sit around and wait all week for it to happen, when they could do it themselves in a couple of seconds.

1

Basins are no longer just vitreous china. They can be glass, stainless steel, even stone. Aren't we fashionable these days!

2

Don't forget the stopper! Clean the plug. White spirit works well on rubber stoppers. A neat way to store the plug is to sit it tidily in the flat overflow slot rather than draping it round the tap, where it always gets in the way.

3

Rub baby oil or bath oil on the bottom of your soap dish to prevent the soap sticking to it.

4

Clean your basin every day, removing soap scum, limescale and germs.

5

To remove limescale from heavily encrusted taps (note that this method is not suitable for plated taps of any kind, especially gold): mix equal parts of white vinegar and water and scrub on with a soft toothbrush. For heavy caking, soak paper towels, wrap around the tap in a plastic bag held in place with an elastic band, and leave overnight. In the morning remove it and the limescale comes clean away!

6

Paint the bottom of metal shaving-foam cans with a little clear nail varnish to stop them leaving rusty ring marks.

7

Gloopy toothbrush mugs are a haven for bacteria. Pop them in the dishwasher once a week to keep them fresh.

We swear shiny taps are good for the soul

How clean is your bidet?

Posh houses and hotels have these bidets, and they're a jolly good idea. Do you know, they have another good use too? After a long day you think, 'Oh, my dogs are barking,' and you can fill up the bidet and soak your feet at a nice manageable height. Lovely!

1 The bidet is normally made of vitreous china, so clean it in the same way as the basin.

2 Keep the spray holes free from limescale with a spray of water and distilled white vinegar. Rinse thoroughly.

3 A little disinfectant keeps the bidet nice and hygienic.

Aren't you the continental one, dear?

Give your pipes a treat!

Once a month, pour a kettleful of boiling water over a cupful of washing soda crystals down each of the plugholes. It will clear away grease and soap residue and leave drains running freely.

CLEANING CLOTHS IN THE BATHROOM

1 Use different-coloured cloths for different jobs to avoid cross-contamination.

2 Use different-coloured cloths for basins and baths from the ones you use for bidets and toilets.

3 Wash and replace all cloths frequently, or use disposable cloths.

Oh, the
grot!

How dusty is your bathroom?

Doesn't the bathroom get dusty quickly?
Vigorous towelling dry produces fluff from
towels and of course lots of dead skin. It's
called dander, but it's not very dandy when
it's allowed to collect on the windowsill, the
floor, the shelves, and all the bottles of potions
and lotions. So use a barely damp cloth to
scoop up all the dust on a regular basis. Who
wants a display of dust? If you have a nice
bowl or ornament in the bathroom, give it
the occasional wash in warm soapy water
to keep it sparkling.

bathroom

TOWELS

Using dark-coloured towels is no excuse not to launder them frequently, just because the dirt doesn't show, you can still smell them, you know! Towels should be changed at least twice a week. The trouble with new towels is they pill. No matter how good the quality, fluff comes off in the wash, so you can't mix them in with your other garments – who wants fluff on their T-shirts? But you don't want to run the machine for just a couple of towels, so splash out – buy half a dozen at a time and wash them all together.

1 Instead of dumping towels in a heap on the floor, spread them out neatly on a rail to dry. Micro-organisms flourish in wet towels.

2 Change your towels at least twice a week.

3 Wash with biological washing powder at 60°C to kill germs and bacteria.

4 Don't share towels.

5 Change hand towels daily.

6 Never put a damp coloured towel in the wash basket, you could dye your other clothes. Pop it into a plastic bag first.

7 Fresh hand towels or a nice pile of facecloths for visitors to dry their hands on are a welcoming sign you care!

STAR TIP
Natural sponges can be hard and gritty when new. Soak them in cold water until they go soft, then squeeze them dry and cover in hot water for five minutes. Now they're soft and lovely.

How clean is your bathroom floor?

The bathroom floor has to put up with a lot of rough treatment. Why, oh why can't men aim straight? Some of them just can't seem to help pebble-dashing the whole area. Disgusting. That's why you should never have carpet in the bathroom. Have a floor you can wash clean, and do it, dear, don't just think about it. It really doesn't take more than a couple of minutes to keep your floor gleaming.

1 Remove everything standing on the floor bins, plants, towel racks.

2 Vacuum or sweep up all the loose bits, paying careful attention to the areas behind the bathroom fittings.

3 Wash lino, laminated wood and ceramic tiles with warm soapy water, using a floorcloth or mop.

4 Always use fresh water for different rooms to stop cross-contamination.

5 Use a different cloth or mop from the one you use for the kitchen floor.

6 For a beautiful shine, buff dry with a soft cloth or an old dry towel.

MIRRORS

Bathroom mirrors will always need polishing.
Condensation leaves them smeary. Toothpaste
splatters are another annoying thing – do you
have a splatterer in your home? And don't you
hate it when the men scrub a patch to see
themselves shave? A good trick is to join them
at their own game. Rub a little shaving foam all
over the mirror and polish off – would you believe
it, the mirror won't steam up next time.

Achieve a shine without tears and smears by using a soft cloth with a little methylated spirit.

A little white vinegar, buffed with paper towels, always produces a pleasing result.

A coffee-filter paper is ideal for buffing, as it doesn't leave any lint behind.

If your mirror becomes dull from hairspray, wipe it over with a little rubbing alcohol to remove the build-up and buff.

Oh, we saw some shockers on our travels, and gasp, the honk! You'll smell bad enough when you're a corpse, so why smell bad when you're alive, for goodness sake? Stinking bedsheets had been clinging grimly to mattresses for months. Duvets were abandoned in a heap, never folded, never washed! Crumbs in the bed, stains on the pillows, greasy fingerprints on the headboard. It wasn't only dust mites that had been happily munching in these sheets. There was no wanting or longing in these beds. Nights of passion were definitely out.

Sticky coffee rings on bedside tables, half-eaten takeaways – yes, honestly, in the bedroom of all places. Mouldy loaves of bread, teacups growing green and furry, drinks cans strewn across every surface.

We clambered over mounds of stinky, dirty, festering clothes erupting like Vesuvius. Clothing spewed out of drawers, wardrobes, every orifice, frequently there was more clothing without than within any furniture designed to contain it. Black bin bags were crammed with dirty laundry. Windows were thick with blackened filth, mould and mildew growing alarmingly across the sills.

And what on earth was that on the floor? In fact, what wasn't on the floor? Toenail clippings, human hair where a man had shaved his head (pushed into a heap and hidden behind a mirror), cat hair, wriggling carpet beetles – it was enough to make you retch. When we tipped up beds we found more junk squirrelled away out of sight – pens, socks, pants, coins – and fluff, lots and lots of fluff, a banquet for the dust mites.

Of course you don't want to live like this. We spend about eight hours asleep every night, so let's be clean and comfortable. You want to spend your hours of slumber in a haven of tranquillity, sleeping soundly and dreaming fondly. Let's make the boudoir a room of beauty. Let's get cleaning!

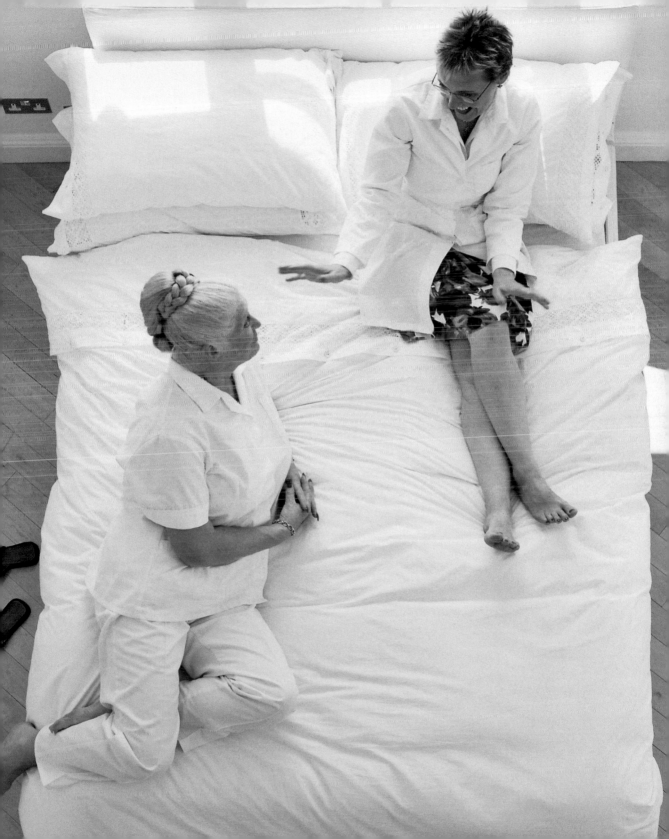

Dust
is the biggest problem in the bedroom

GRIME FILE
Dust mites love your bedroom. It's warm, humid, and when you're in bed you're shedding skin flakes, so they have a constant supply of food. Aren't we the generous ones? We each perspire half a litre of water into our beds and bedroom air each night.

The dust mite is very small – shorter than the width of a strand of hair. It's a good job we can't see them, or we'd never climb into bed. Dust mites secure themselves to the fibres of our bedding and mattresses with the claws on each of their eight legs. As they digest our skin flakes they secrete guanine, which contains dust mite saliva and excrement. It's this microscopic dust that can cause health problems such as asthma, bronchitis, eczema, itchy eyes and a stuffy nose.

Dust mites can be controlled with effective cleaning.

This is especially important for people who are susceptible to allergies exacerbated by dust. Laundering your bed linen, under-blanket, pillowcases, duvets and pillows at 60°C will kill dust mites and remove their faeces. Cooler water will remove the allergens but it won't kill the mites. Regular vacuuming – and don't forget under the bed   is also an important weapon in the fight against dust mites. Suck up as much dust and fluff as you can, and don't forget to change the vacuum bag regularly.

You should also do your best to keep heat and humidity below the levels which support mites: temperature under 21°C and relative humidity below 45 per cent. Leaving a window open at night helps achieve both, and airing the bedding and the room in the morning also plays a big part in keeping down humidity.

bedroom

Don't swish dust, dear – lift it!

Dust is a devil, isn't it? No matter how fastidious you are it soon comes back. Swishing it round will only make matters worse, so don't swish, dear – lift it. Get friendly with your vacuum and use your duster slightly damp.

HOW TO DUST

1 Regular vacuuming is the most effective way to remove dust without making it airborne again.

2 Use your duster slightly damp. Take a clean one, rinse it under the tap and then wring out as tightly as possible. The dust is attracted to the dampness, so it is picked up rather than moved around.

3 Use a lambswool or anti-static feather duster to collect cobwebs and dust from hard-to-reach places.

4 Don't forget your lampshades. Drag your very slightly damp duster over the surface, gathering the dust towards you. If the dust is stubborn, flick the damp duster firmly over the surface.

How clean is your bed?

Who wants to climb into a dirty, pongy bed at the
end of a long tiring day? Sweet dreams are unlikely
if we're sandwiched between smelly sheets. When
we're tucked up lovely and snug we don't half perspire,
you know, so air your bed, dear. In the morning pull
back the covers and let the bed breathe. Change the
sheets once a week, please (twice a week in warm
weather) – we don't want to be doing the sniff test
on your stinky bedding.

Keep your mattress and pillows covered – we're all
dribblers, you know. And for heaven's sake don't
be a lazybones. if you turn your mattress regularly
it will repay you with kindness and, if you're lucky,
nights of passion!

FOR A NIGHT TO REMEMBER . . .

1 Keep your mattress clean. Use a mattress protector and launder it once a month.

2 Always follow the manufacturer's instructions on how to care for your mattress.

3 Remove marks from the mattress by using upholstery cleaner, or dilute a drop of concentrated washing-up liquid in a bowl of water. Whisk rapidly and then use just the suds on a sponge to remove marks. Pat the mattress dry using a towel.

4 Another way to freshen the mattress is to sprinkle bicarbonate of soda on it to absorb musty odours. Leave it for a couple of hours and then vacuum off.

5 Turn your mattress over once a month, rotating the ends to give the mattress a chance to recover its shape. This is especially important if two people of different sizes are sharing the same bed.

6 Vacuum the mattress every couple of months, using low suction and the crevice tool.

7 Hang bedcovers and quilts outside to air. Use pillow protectors under your pillowcases, and launder them monthly.

8 Most duvets can be washed – look at the label. If your washing machine drum isn't large enough to accommodate your duvet, take it to the launderette, where the wash capacity is larger.

9 Many pillows, even feather ones, can be laundered. Check the label for washing instructions. Wash pillows twice a year to freshen and remove dust mite residue.

10 To dry feather and down pillows or duvets back to their original fluffy state, add between two and six clean tennis balls to the drier. The beating action will bring them back to life beautifully.

11 Change your sheets at least once a week. Wash at 60°C to kill dust mites and remove their faeces.

12 Add some of your favourite bath salts to the final rinse for wonderfully fragranced sheets.

13 Fold sheets in half to dry and hang up carefully – they will be much easier to iron. Iron sheets while they are still slightly damp for a much more pleasing finish.

14 If you like your guest beds to be made up all the time, keep them smelling fresh by placing a fabric softener sheet under the blanket or quilt until the bed is needed.

15 Headboards should also be kept clean and fresh. Polish wood; for laminates use a cream cleanser; for upholstery, vacuum using the upholstery nozzle or a soft brush attachment. For removing marks from upholstered headboards, use the same method as for cleaning a mattress

16 If you need to store things under your bed, use plastic storage trays with lids or cotton covers. The stiff cardboard fruit trays that you can pick up from supermarkets are a good cost-free alternative, but make lids for them to keep out dust. You need to be able to slide out the storage containers regularly for vacuuming underneath the bed.

bedroom

How clean is your wardrobe?

If you want to store old clothes for 10 years, expect to have a horrible time. You know your clothes: if you don't wear half of them, why not give them to someone who will? Don't be stingy, invest in some nice shapely hangers that will suspend your garments with grace – those wire ones from the dry-cleaners really won't do. Keep your wardrobe well ventilated. You can help avoid dampness and fustiness in wardrobes if you spread your clothes so that air can pass between them, and please avoid returning to the wardrobe grubby stuff that will not only pong the place out, but will also attract moths.

1 Cramming clothes into wardrobes will not only make them harder to find, they crease and may attract textile pests, mould and mildew if the air cannot circulate freely.

2 Make space in your wardrobes by packing your out-of-season clothes in suitcases or storage bags when you are not using them.

3 At the beginning of each season as you exchange the two collections of clothes you will be able to see everything that you have, and decide what new things you need to buy.

4 If you have clothes you haven't worn for two years it is highly likely that you will never wear them again. Pass them on to someone else who can make use of them, or send them to a charity shop.

Hang cedar bark or sachets of dried lavender in wardrobes to discourage moths. It is the larvae, not the moths, that eat the clothes.

Store woollens in zippable plastic storage bags to help prevent moths laying eggs in them.

Keep items that tend to form mildew – for example shoes and suitcases – on racks or shelves with holes, to allow the air to circulate freely around them.

Allow clothes that have been worn to air before returning them to the wardrobe. The moisture transferred from your body to the clothes may cause mould if the clothes are put away before they have aired.

Avoid returning heavily soiled clothes to wardrobes. It is the human bacterial remains in textiles that most attract textile pests.

Place a charcoal briquette in each corner of the wardrobe (or any area where damp occurs) to keep mildew away. The briquette will absorb the moisture which the mildew needs to survive.

US PAT #
4930272

Less mess,
more rest

How clean are your drawers?

Oh, the joy of opening a well-ordered drawer! Everything in its place, no need to rummage or curse – just go straight to what you're looking for! Doesn't that sound like heaven? And it's so easy to do! It only takes a minute to keep things well ordered, so start today, don't put it off until tomorrow, start now. Do it, dear!

Just as with wardrobes, it is useful to clear out the contents from time to time.

Try to do a drawer every month: that way you'll keep on top of clutter rather than saving it up.

If you can fit things easily into drawers and cupboards you are more likely to put them away. Untidiness makes cleaning more difficult and leads to dust and dirt accumulating.

Try to maintain order over which drawer contains what, so that returning things to their place is easier and quicker.

Discard items you no longer use.

An easy way to vacuum drawers without blocking the vacuum hose with pins and loose buttons is to pop a pair of tights or a stocking over the nozzle.

Using drawer-lining paper helps keep drawers and clothes clean. You can also use wallpaper remnants as a cheap and pretty lining paper to match your decor. Scented paper keeps clothes smelling sweet.

How clean are your curtains and blinds?

The bedroom is one room where you will want to cover the windows – we don't want the neighbours to see us in the altogether, do we? Drab drapes are very 'during the war', dear.

Curtains should be shaken and vacuumed frequently to remove dust and keep them clean. If you have floor-length curtains, pay special attention to the hems where dirt from the floor collects.

Wipe your windowsills regularly with warm soapy water. Mildew tends to form around bedroom windows, especially when they are closed during the winter and condensation gets trapped. You don't want this to transfer to your precious curtains.

Launder or dry-clean curtains as appropriate. Allowing fabric to get very dirty tends to make cleaning much less successful.

Roller blinds can be vacuumed using the upholstery attachment. If the blind is waterproof, sponge it, using upholstery shampoo.

Venetian blinds are very popular, but don't they collect a lot of dust! Remove the dust regularly. Wear a pair of cotton house gloves and run your fingers along each slat, picking up the dust as you go. It's much less fiddly than using a duster.

A quicker method is to rotate all the slats to the upward angle, wipe with a damp duster or vacuum using a soft brush attachment, then reverse the slats and repeat.

How clean is your floor?

Housework is good for the figure, it really is. Did you know that throwing round the vacuum or mop will burn up to 200 calories an hour? Tell them that at your next slimming class and they'll all want spotless homes!

CARPETS

In Britain fully fitted carpets have always been popular in bedrooms, but the carpet is the largest reservoir of dust in the home. Human hair and skin cells, pet hair and skin, food debris and dirt from shoes are all embedded in the average carpet. Needless to say, dust mites find the residue in carpets very attractive. A home with bare boards and a few rugs may well have a tenth of the dust of a home with wall-to-wall fitted carpets.

Vacuum the carpet in the bedroom at least once a week. Don't just vacuum the centre of the room and round the bed, but go up to the edges and into corners. Use the crevice nozzle attachment if necessary.

Avoid laying rugs on top of carpet – they will gradually wear away the weave in the carpet underneath.

At least once a month vacuum under the bed, preferably by pulling the bed right out and giving the area a good working over.

WOODEN FLOORS

Varnished and sealed wooden laminate floors can be kept clean and free of dust with a barely damp mop, after vacuuming or sweeping up loose particles. Excess water can damage protective coatings.

Try to avoid mangling the fringe of rugs. Don't push the vacuum cleaner backwards and forwards, but pull it back towards yourself, drawing the tassels outwards.

Microfibre flat-surface mops are also an effective innovation. Run over the floor in a gentle curving 'S' shape to pick up dust, they can also be used damp. The cleaning pads can be removed and washed in the washing machine.

I like to vacuum myself out of the door, so it's lovely and fresh when I get back

How clean is your laundry basket?

At the end of each day pop your used clothes into a basket with a lid. Don't leave them scattered over the floor and furniture.

Get into the habit of sorting through your laundry every couple of days and popping a load into the machine.

Consider using different baskets or divided sections for whites, lights, coloureds and delicates.

Don't leave clothes to fester at the bottom of the basket for months on end – they will attract textile beetles and moths, which feed on the human bacteria remains in soiled garments.

STAR TIP
Pop a fabric softener sheet in the basket to keep it smelling fresh.

How clean are your children's rooms?

Children's rooms can be a constant headache. Children tend not to appreciate tidiness with the same relish as you, but you can set a good example, both in your room and theirs! Of course you shouldn't let your fastidiousness get in the way of their creativity, but try to encourage them to clear up before moving on to the next activity.

KEEPING TOYS TIDY

Store toys in a wooden toybox, or in plastic stackable boxes with lids. Use different colours for different types of toys, or to denote which toys are whose.

Encourage children to return their toys to the boxes at the end of the day so that floors and surfaces are easier to keep clean.

KEEPING TOYS FREE FROM GERMS

Toys can become contaminated with bacteria and viruses when children handle them, or put them to their mouths.

Plastic toys can be washed in warm soapy water from time to time to keep them fresh. Plastic toys can also go in the dishwasher on a normal wash cycle.

Put soft toys (check the washing instructions) inside a pillowcase, tie a knot in the top and pop into the washing machine on a delicate wash cycle.

You can freshen soft toys by popping them into a paper sack with a little bicarbonate of soda and shaking gently. Leave for a couple of hours, then vacuum the powder away gently.

If soft toys cannot be washed, wipe over the pile gently with a very slightly damp soapy cloth, followed by a clean cloth. Dry with a hairdryer if necessary.

Mucky masterpieces

Ooh, children can be little terrors at times – their idea
of creativity can lead to all kinds of cleaning headaches!
But don't despair – you can mop up their masterpieces
effortlessly with a little bit of know-how!

REMOVING STICKERS, CRAYON AND CHEWING-GUM

To remove adhesive stickers from
paintwork, tear off the paper
surface and spray the sticky residue
with oil lubricant (WD40). Allow to
soak, then wipe away with paper
towels. Attack stubborn marks
with a plastic scraper.

To remove crayon from radiators,
rub with a paper towel soaked in
milk from the fridge.

To get crayon off carpet, scrape
off as much as possible with a knife,
then put several layers of paper
towel over the mark and press
lightly with a warm iron. The towel
soaks up the waxy residue.

To remove chewing-gum from
carpet and fabric, rub with an ice
cube inside a plastic bag until the
gum goes brittle and then lift off.

pets and allergies

We met some wonderful people on our travels – despite the filth they were living in! We also got acquainted with a variety of cats and dogs that definitely ruled the roost. They had very kindly marked out their territories to make sure the owners knew who was boss. And oh, the honk! As soon as we stepped over the threshold we were gassed by the foul stench of damp dog, or stale cat, and sometimes both! The worst whiff of stale doggie whatsits that greeted us was in a house where the owners didn't even have a dog, but had been visited by one that had left an everlasting gift.

Journeying further into these homes, we quickly realized that living with pets isn't always healthy for the domestically challenged. Animal hair is best on animals, not on sofas, beds, curtains, carpets, skirtings – even in the fridge! These filth furballs certainly made us want to retch. Please keep your pets off the beds and sofas, and if you must share your most intimate spaces with them, make your vacuum cleaner your next best friend.

Stinky sofas were proof that the pets were more at home in the living room than their owners. And the bed really is no place for the family dog. Who knows what's lurking in that coat? The human occupants would certainly find out come bedtime. Kitchens were the prime grime scenes in these homes. We saw half-eaten bowls of festering food, and cat-litter trays teeming with unmentionables. There were pools of pee-pee and piles of poops; now that's just not healthy where people are eating.

Please, we're both ever so fond of our four-legged and feathered friends. They're our faithful companions and we wouldn't be without them – but if you don't clean those fluffy balls of fun, you'll soon be surrounded by ferocious filth.

Stale poopy doops and pee-pees — banish them!

Man's best friend

They're cuddly, adorable and our favourite companions, but domestic moggies and doggies, along with more exotic fashionable species, can carry bacteria harmful to humans. Your pet may look healthy but can also be a carrier of salmonella, campylobacter, helminths (tapeworms), protozoa (toxoplasmosis, toxocariasis) and viruses (rabies). These are carried in their faeces, saliva, coats and skin – dog faeces have been found to carry up to 30 diseases that affect humans.

All these germs can be transferred to humans through licking, stroking, biting and scratching. If pets are allowed to roam freely around the neighbourhood, they can pick up all sorts of bacteria on their paws and bring them back into the home. If pets are given free rein in the home too, they may increase levels of contamination in the kitchen and bathroom, where good hygiene is important for human health.

HOW TO AVOID CONTAMINATION FROM CATS AND DOGS

Pets should be appropriately immunized against disease. If your pet doesn't look well, get it to a vet as soon as possible.

Hands should always be washed after touching any pet, pet cages, pet-feeding utensils and pet playthings.

Never let pets eat from family plates or walk on surfaces where food is prepared. Any surfaces a pet may have been in contact with should be thoroughly cleaned before food preparation.

The kitchen is not a suitable room in which to house or feed pets.

Don't clean pet cages and tanks in the kitchen sink – they could transfer harmful bacteria to food preparation areas. Clean them outside if possible, or use the bath and clean it thoroughly afterwards.

Floor surfaces used by pets, and pet-feeding areas, should be regularly decontaminated, using an anti-bacterial cleaner.

Pet urine, faeces and vomit should be cleaned up immediately and contaminated surfaces cleaned and disinfected.

Litter trays should never be kept in the kitchen. They should be emptied on a daily basis.

Pregnant women should avoid cleaning cat-litter trays, as cats harbour toxoplasmosis, a germ that can harm unborn babies.

If you suffer from allergies, keep pets off beds and preferably out of the bedroom altogether. Pets should have beds of their own – not share with their owners.

pets and allergies

Kim's feline friend – Daisy

I've always loved cats: they're marvellous, great fun, and if you're good to them they'll give a lot of affection back. Enjoy your pets, talk to them, stroke them, cherish them, and please give them a jolly good brush!

My Daisy is a sweet little soul; she really is a gem. She's been living with my husband and me for a year now; she's a house cat, a simple little moggie, but fully house-trained. Still, I don't let her out of my sight. After she's had a twinkle or done a number two, she doesn't wash herself immediately, so I make sure she's not padding towards my bedroom to make herself comfortable on my bed until she's thoroughly cleaned her intimate parts.

If you can train a cat to twinkle in a tray you can also train it to keep off surfaces used for food preparation – you won't find my Daisy sticking her head in the mixing bowl. Start training when they're kittens. Daisy's only one but she's grown up enough to know her place.

Pussycats by their nature want to go out, and my Daisy's the same – I do let her go outside but she doesn't go far, so I know where's she's been. But if you're out at work, you can't be sure where your pet's been and what they've picked up along the way, so you really do need to clean them more frequently. Cats are constantly grooming themselves and are considered to be clean creatures, rather like myself – but I'm not constantly licking my fur and shedding it around the house.

Don't have an animal unless you've got the time, dear. They do need attention. Also mind cats around little ones – don't be too trusting with any pet when children are around.

The key to cleaning up after pets is the same as with any cleaning: do it as it happens, and you'll have more time to enjoy their company.

Aggie's family and their feathered friends

I agree with Kim that having a pet is a big responsibility – as if you haven't got enough cleaning to do already. If you have a family, pets also present another area for argument – who's going to walk them, groom them, clean up their mess, and feed them?

My boys nagged us to get a pet. Finally we gave in and compromised with a pair of canaries, which need much less maintenance than cats or dogs. Of course there's still mess to deal with: birdseed gets flicked all over the place, and if it's not cleaned up it can attract mice and other pests.

Bird droppings may pale into significance beside cat poo, but it's still full of bacteria so you need to clean the cage regularly. Our cage is quite large, so I only clean it once a week, but smaller cages should be cleaned more often. My son Rory is meant to take full responsibility for the birds but claims his squeamishness prevents him from fulfilling his duties so we have struck a deal: he sets the birds free in the playroom, brings the cage outside and assembles all the necessary paraphernalia. I always clean the cage outside, no matter how cold it is. I put on rubber gloves, scoop the contents of the cage into a carrier bag, and dispose of it in the dustbin. Then I hose the cage down a couple of times and dry it thoroughly – because birds don't like the damp. Next I scrub the perches and all the other toys in the cage. Finally I put some clean sandpaper in the bottom of the cage, which helps the birds digest their food.

It's a good idea to let birds spread their wings now and again, but they are then at liberty to wee and poo, so cover any upholstery or expensive rugs. And of course always keep windows and doors closed. When the weather's fine, we take the cage out into the garden to give the birds a change of scene. They love it, and it's a good opportunity to air the house – because however clean your birds are, they provide their own scent.

Living with cats and dogs – teaching them new tricks

Pets need to know who's boss: where they can hang out, and where they can't. The kitchen isn't a suitable home for dog baskets and cat-litter trays. Nor should pets be allowed to share your dishes or roam over surfaces where food is prepared. It is also important that reptiles and birds should not be kept where food is prepared – they can carry diseases harmful to humans.

You will certainly need to vacuum and dust more often and more thoroughly – just think about the hair being shed, the litter trays, fleas, a little accident here and there – and the risk to health, not to mention the unpleasant honk that will follow if you don't. You will also need to wash hard floors more frequently, and shampoo carpets regularly.

Pets can carry diseases and germs. If you allow your pets outside, keep some old towels handy to wipe their paws when they come back into the house.

Along with the fur, dander is constantly shed. This may cause an allergic reaction in some people. If a member of the household has any kind of allergy to dust, keep pets out of the bedrooms.

Cleaner pets mean a cleaner house. Bathe and brush cats and dogs regularly to minimize the amount of pet hair and dander (dead skin flakes) they shed and to help combat odours. Always do this outside.

Pet hair clings to everything and can be a devil to get rid of. Always keep a lint brush, pet rake (a brush that has crimped nylon bristles) or damp sponge handy to pick up stray pet hair.

Vacuum thoroughly at least twice a week. Standard vacuum cleaners don't always pick up all the hair. Consider investing in one of the specialist models that have a high-powered turbo brush attachment designed specifically to lift animal hair from carpet and rugs.

To clean up pet vomit, sprinkle with bicarbonate of soda, allow it to be absorbed, and then vacuum or scoop up. Follow up with a carpet stain-remover and rinse with warm water with a couple of drops of antiseptic.

To remove hair from fabric and upholstery, use a chamois leather wrung dry. Drag the cloth towards you and you'll gather all the hair together with it. If dampness will harm the fabric, as in the case of velour, try using the rubber sole of a clean training shoe, or a rubber glove.

A light mist of spray-on vegetable oil on feeding bowls will make them easier to wash out. This will also help stop pets' skins drying out and reduce flaking dander.

pets and allergies

How clean is your cat-litter tray?

Picture it – they're in the tray doing their thing, pooping and peeing. This attracts flies, which are also soon doing their business. Then your cat jumps up on the worktop, into the sink, licking your crockery, tongue around the taps, padding across the clean draining-board. It's not a pretty image, is it?

Cats can be carriers of enteric pathogens such as campylobacter and salmonella – the most common causes of food poisoning. These can cause diarrhoea, cramping, abdominal pain and fever – not nice! These harmful bacteria can be transferred to humans via contact with infected faecal matter from a sickly cat or dog. Litter trays and kitchens don't mix. It's a pet hate, excuse the pun, for both of us. So get that litter tray out of the kitchen now!

1 Rule number 1 – never keep a litter tray in the kitchen. Choose a cool shaded area that is well ventilated, avoiding living areas where possible.

2 Faecal matter should be removed from the surface of the litter as soon as you see it. Using gloved hands, scoop up the faeces with bathroom tissue and flush it down the loo. Don't put it in the bin. Faeces of any kind should not be left in the house in any shape or form.

3 Empty litter trays daily, or at the very least every other day. Dispose of litter carefully in an outside receptacle and disinfect the tray with a diluted bleach solution.

4 Cats are twinkling all the time, and it's absorbed into the litter. Just because you can't see it doesn't mean you can ignore it. It'll soon start stinking.

STAR TIP
To keep the litter smelling fresh and fragrant, sprinkle some bicarbonate of soda in the bottom of the tray before you put the litter in.

A flea in your ear

There are around 2,000 species of fleas worldwide and the most common is the cat flea. These small, wingless, ecto-parasitic insects have been the scourge of many households for years.

These fleas aren't particularly fussy about who their host is, and it's likely that your poor doggie is carrying cat fleas around too. However, the fleas actually only live on the animal for about three days, during which time they're laying between 15 and 20 eggs a day each. These eggs are falling on to the carpet, the sofa, the bed, into all the corners – anywhere your pet roams.

Pet owners spend a fortune on flea-collars and powders but there's little point spraying the animals if you're not cleaning as well. The only way to stop fleas thriving is to get rid of those eggs, because after a few days, they hatch.

1 Thoroughly and regularly clean areas where adult fleas, flea larvae and eggs are found. Vacuum floors, rugs, carpets, upholstered furniture, pet bedding and crevices around skirting boards daily, or at least every other day.

2 Flea eggs can survive and grow inside vacuum cleaner bags. Get rid of bags immediately by sealing them inside a plastic sack and placing them in a covered rubbish bin outside the home, or put a flea collar in the bottom of the bag to prevent them nesting and breeding.

3 Kitty owners frequently become immune to flea-bites and are unaware that there is a problem. Visitors end up suffering the most, but are usually too polite to mention the problem to their host. You'll only know you have a problem when people stop calling round!

4 In rural retreats, a sweet little moggy may pick up rat, rabbit or hedgehog fleas and bring them into the home – how lovely. They might give you a sharp nip, but unlike the cat flea, they won't set up home indoors.

pets and allergies

CAT HAIR AND COMPUTERS

Kitties love anywhere warm and cosy, and the hum of a working computer makes it a very desirable place to rest their weary heads, bless 'em. In homes where cats prowl, computer air vents have been found to contain an inch of thick hair and fluff inside the casing, and this snug nest can soon play home to other insects. Wayward pet fur can also get inside the disk or CD drive and cause problems such as skipping CDs or unreadable disks.

If your cat sheds fur on the keyboard you should clean it frequently. Before cleaning it, turn off the keyboard and disconnect the keyboard from the PC. You can blow out a lot of the cat hair, along with the crumbs and dust, with a hairdryer or a can of compressed air. Use compressed air to blast out detritus from the drives as well as from its air vents.

If your computer is exceedingly clogged up, call in a computer specialist to dismantle the hard-drive and monitor and give it a thorough clean.

OOH, THE HONK – KEEP YOUR CATS AND DOGS SMELLING FRESH

Let's face it, pets have a unique odour that clings to everything and can quickly take over the whole home. Commercial air fresheners are expensive, and contain ingredients that can be harmful to the environment and your pets. Air freshener will only mask the pong, not neutralize it.

1. A really stinky cat or dog may mean it has a skin disease and should be checked out by a vet.

2. Let your pets out as often as possible. It will keep them happy and healthy and your home will stand a better chance of smelling fresh.

3. Deodorize your cat or dog by rubbing bicarbonate of soda into its coat and then brushing it off. This will clean the coat too.

4. Vacuum and launder all pet bedding twice weekly.

5. To freshen and deodorize upholstery, carpets and pet bedding, liberally sprinkle on bicarbonate of soda. Wait 15 minutes or longer depending on strength of odour, then vacuum.

6. Combine one part distilled white vinegar to five parts water. Pour into a spray bottle and spray into odorous areas. You can also spray in places you don't want your pets to go – they don't like vinegar.

STAR TIP
Don't use ammonia or ammonia-based products to clean up cat accidents. The cats identify the smell as close to their own and will re-offend again.

DOGGIE DO-DOS AND DOGGIE DON'TS . . .

It's important to train dogs to go outside when they want to do their business. But no matter how well trained your dog is, there will be accidents from time to time. When dogs urinate, the stain is only part of the problem, it's the stinky odour that marks their territory, and keeps these grime offenders coming back and re-offending on the same spot if you don't do something about it.

1 With any accident, move quickly before the urine has soaked through. Limit absorption by applying paper towels. After absorbing as much as possible, dilute the spot first using a cloth dampened with cold water or soda water, then clean with an acid solution of three parts soda water to one part white vinegar. Finish cleaning with an ammonia solution (1–10 ratio with water), then rinse.

2 For older stains, add a small amount of washing up liquid to a bucket of warm water and one cap of chlorine bleach or household ammonia and apply with a clean cloth. Next cover with a dry white towel or disposable kitchen towel and do the dance of joy on the towel to absorb the moisture.

3 Distilled white vinegar sprayed on the spot also removes identifying odours, and dogs no longer recognize the territory as their own.

4 If the spot has seen multiple accidents, the bacteria breaking down the stain may actually create a concentrated alkaline state that interferes with the enzyme digester's effectiveness. Not all is lost. After the bacteria digester has been working for about four hours, neutralize the spot by mixing a solution of one cup vinegar to a gallon of warm water. Rinse the area with vinegar solution. Finally. apply a fresh batch of bacteria/ enzyme digester solution.

5 If the pong persists it means the urine has got into the carpet backing or pad and there is no practical way to clean this. No amount of deodorizing will mask the lingering stench – a new carpet might be the solution, or buy a hypodermic needle from a chemist and fill it with your favourite perfume. You'll need to inject both the carpet and pad for it to work.

STAR TIP
Use biological washing powder containing enzymes to break down ammonia in pet urine and neutralize odour, or enzyme digesters (from pet shops) to banish the smells. Read fabric labels to check enzyme digesters can be used.

BIRDS AND REPTILES

1 Exotic reptiles such as iguanas and turtles have become very popular as pets, but they can be carriers of salmonella so it's very important to wash your hands after handling. Salmonella transfers easily to every surface you touch, and can lead to severe stomach upsets and diarrhoea. Younger children are especially at risk from infections carried by animals because their immune systems are less developed. Children don't always understand the importance of good hygiene, so you need to explain the risks to them clearly and get them into the habit of washing their hands.

2 Don't allow pet reptiles to roam freely in the home. Reptiles should not be kept in kitchens.

3 Children under five should avoid contact with reptiles; older children should be taught to practise safe hygiene. Hands should always be washed thoroughly with soap and water after handling reptiles and their cages.

4 Kitchen sinks should not be used for bathing reptiles or washing their dishes, cages or aquariums. Clean the tank in the bathroom sink or tub and make sure to clean the tub afterwards with 1 part household bleach to 10 parts water.

5 Psittacosis (parrot fever) is an infectious disease transmitted to humans from birds in the parrot family. Inhaling dust from dried droppings of birdcages spreads the disease. The droppings can remain infectious for weeks.

6 If birds are kept as pets, clean the cage often so that faeces do not accumulate, because as they dry they become airborne.

Is your pet making you sick?

Apart from leaving hair all over the house and adding to your dust problem, pets are also constantly shedding dander, the old skin scales which, like dead human skin cells, provide extra fodder for the feasting mites. Dogs and cats are the most common sources of animal allergens, but almost any furry or feathered friend, from hamsters to budgies, can trigger allergies.

If you are sensitive to animal dander, wear an allergy-proof face mask when grooming animals and while vacuuming. If possible delegate the task to someone else.

If you have pets, keep bedroom doors closed. Don't let them wander into the bedroom. Definitely don't let pets share your bed. Inevitably they will shed hair and skin particles which will exacerbate allergic reactions.

Thoroughly vacuum pet bedding daily and anywhere else your pet spends time. Allowing pets to sit on soft furnishings creates extra work.

Keep litter trays, bedding and cages in a well-ventilated room or area.

If possible, let your pet outside for part of the day. Take bird and hamster cages outdoors when the weather is fine. This will help keep the levels of animal dander, and the smell, down. Your pet will appreciate the change of scene too.

After touching or playing with pets always wash your hands, and wash clothes in the hottest wash the care instructions will allow.

pets and allergies

Is your home making you sick?

One of the excuses we encountered for not cleaning was that housework literally made people feel sick. Chemicals from cleaning fluids, and the disturbance of dust, make some people feel so ill that they avoid cleaning altogether. Little do they know that they are actually making themselves feel worse by shirking their duties.

An increasing number of people – estimated as high as 40 per cent – are prone to asthma, and there is strong evidence that household dust exacerbates the condition. The best way to avoid the shortness of breath, watery eyes and itchy nose that people complain of when cleaning is to do it more often and use gentler cleaning products.

The homes we visited had windows jammed firmly shut, central heating on full blast and the dust mites were having a ball. High temperatures and high humidity are ideal breeding conditions for these brutes, and it is the enzymes in their faeces that can cause an allergic reaction. One home we called at was so dirty the poor lass was wheezing and breathless; however, two weeks later a clean home had not only lifted her spirits – but her asthma had improved. We're not doctors, but we know what's good for you!

Dust wasn't the only problem. One lad's bedroom was literally mouldy and green with lack of cleaning and ventilation. Living like this certainly isn't healthy. No wonder he wasn't sharing his love nest with any young ladies. We hope his love life has perked up since we sorted him out.

Some cleaning materials do contain harsh ingredients, but there are plenty of effective alternatives. So if cleaning is making you sick, we've got bags of jolly good practical advice for you. Let's get cleaning!

GRIME FILE

When people claim they are allergic to housework, this may not be too far from the truth. Many allergy sufferers, especially asthmatics, are sensitive to allergens contained in house dust. An allergen is a protein that some people react to by producing allergic antibodies. These antibodies trigger allergic reactions including asthma, eczema, rhinitis and hay fever. There are several types of allergens to be found in the home, including those from cats, dogs and moulds.

The biggest nuisance by far is the house dust mite, which feeds off human skin cells, pet dander and other debris found in dust. To most people dust mites are not a problem, but the allergen that is excreted in their faeces is believed to be one of the most common triggers of asthma. It is estimated that 85 per cent of asthma sufferers are allergic to dust mite allergens. These allergens can also cause stuffy and runny noses, and dermatitis.

Dust mites thrive in warm, humid environments, and our cosy modern centrally heated houses, with fitted carpets, double glazing and draught-proof doors, not only make a perfect home for you, but create a snug guesthouse in which dust mites happily thrive.

If you think your home is making you sick, or if there's an allergy sufferer in your household, use some good old common sense to bring about healthy change. Vacuum regularly to remove dust; dust with a barely damp cloth to prevent simply making the dust airborne; and launder clothes and bedlinen regularly.

Aren't you the sensitive sort?

The excuses we had to listen to when we were on our travels! 'Ooh, I can't wash up – it makes my hands go red and wrinkly.' That would explain why we couldn't see their kitchen sinks for overflowing heaps of dirty dishes, covered in slime and going green with mould. As you know well by now, dear, we don't accept any excuses for not cleaning.

GET KITTED OUT FOR THE JOB

1 We often have special protective clothing for gardening and DIY jobs, so why not extend that care to housework? Your skin will appreciate the protection, and your lungs will feel much happier, dear.

2 Wear protective gloves. If rubber gloves don't suit you, try PVC. For tasks that don't involve water, wear surgical latex gloves, or cotton house gloves. If you are sensitive to rubber and PVC, wear a pair of cotton gloves inside a larger size pair. Moisturize your hands before you put on gloves so your hands stay soft.

3 Always wash your hands carefully with a soap-free cleanser to remove any traces of cleaning fluids.

4 Pay special attention to drying your hands: don't allow them to air dry, as the skin will quickly become dry and sore.

5 Wear an allergy-proof face mask when dusting, vacuuming, grooming pets and changing beds.

6 Wear loose-fitting clothes that allow you to move freely and comfortably. Change out of them as soon as you have finished cleaning and put them in the wash.

7 Take a shower after housework to remove dust from your hair and skin.

A breath of fresh air, dear

Sadly, the presence of allergens in the home is not only related to cleanliness. Temperature, humidity and ventilation all play an important part. Optimum conditions for dust mites to breed are temperatures above 70°C, and high levels of humidity – caused by poor ventilation. Open those windows to keep humidity down, keep bedrooms at lower temperatures than living rooms, and please, for heaven's sake, clean!

AN ALLERGY-FRIENDLY CLEANING REGIME

Vacuum thoroughly at least twice a week. For allergy sufferers this requires more than a two-minute dash around the centre of the carpet. Pay attention to the edges of carpets, behind furniture and especially under the bed. Use the vacuum cleaner attachments for upholstery, curtains, mattresses, skirtings and shelves.

If there is an allergy sufferer in your home, consider buying a vacuum cleaner fitted with a HEPA filter (a high-efficiency particulate air filter). All vacuum cleaners return exhaust air back into the room. These filters remove minute dust particles that are not caught inside the bag or cylinder. Look out for a machine with the Allergy UK seal of approval. Remember to change the charcoal filter once a year to keep the air filtration system working effectively.

Wash hard floors with a mild solution of concentrated washing-up liquid. Unsurprisingly, considered its intended use, it is very good at cutting through grease and grime.

Dust with a slightly dampened cloth. This will trap the dust as you work, rather than sending it airborne.

Keep surfaces clean and free from dust. Cut down on clutter and ornaments – they prevent easy cleaning and collect dust.

Walls can also become coated with allergens, and should be vacuumed with a soft brush and washed from time to time.

If you suffer severely from dust mite allergens, consider installing hard floor-coverings such as wooden floors and tiles; leather upholstery will be better for you than fabric types, too. Typically a house with stripped or laminated floorboards and a few rugs will have only a tenth of the dust found in a house with wall-to-wall fitted carpets. The high incidence of asthma in the UK compared to our European neighbours has been linked with our love of carpet, and their preference for wood and tile.

Health is happiness
happiness is a clean home

If your home suffers from high levels of condensation (tell-tale signs are pools of water collecting on windowsills, moisture on painted walls and mildew), installing a dehumidifier may improve matters.

Allergy-friendly cleaning materials

If you suffer from any sort of sensitivity, modern cleaning products with their harsh chemicals can provoke unpleasant reactions in the lungs, eyes and skin. If you notice a reaction to any product, stop using it, because there are bound to be alternatives. A bad reaction is no excuse to stop cleaning altogether. Our grandmothers didn't have the vast array of products we have today; they relied on a small arsenal of kinder, cheaper, more natural cleaners. In those halcyon days, when cleaning was considered an art, the cupboard under the sink contained vinegar, bicarbonate of soda, washing soda crystals, soda water, lemon juice, salt and a big thick bar of soap. If they wanted for much else they didn't know it.

ESSENTIAL ITEMS YOU WON'T FIND IN THE CLEANING AISLE (YET!)

Distilled white vinegar – wonderful for removing limescale, cleaning windows and neutralizing pet odours. Vinegar is acidic, so proceed carefully on delicate surfaces and never use on plated surfaces.

Mix a solution of distilled white vinegar and water (half and half) in a spray bottle. Spray on tiles, basins, baths, mirrors and windows. Rinse thoroughly. Polish dry with a cloth or paper towels. Vinegar cuts through grease, grime, soap scum and limescale and leaves a beautiful shine.

Remove rust and water spots from stainless steel sinks by applying distilled white vinegar with a damp cloth or sponge, then rinse. It will not only erase the spots but will also brighten the sink.

Add half a cup of vinegar to your dishwasher rinse cycle for sparkling and streak-free dishes.

Apply equal parts vinegar and salt to remove coffee and tea stains from the insides of cups.

Bicarbonate of soda – a super cleaner. The mild abrasive properties help to cut through dirt and grease – use it as you would a soft scrubbing product or cleanser in tubs, basins and sinks. It is also an excellent deodorizer.

Make your own non-toxic scouring powder by mixing four parts bicarbonate of soda to one part washing soda crystals. It's easy, cheap, very effective, and kinder on you.

Mix bicarbonate of soda to a paste by adding a little distilled white vinegar – use on stainless steel sinks and drainers for a beautiful clean shine.

To remove stubborn burnt-on food from casserole dishes, fill the dish with hot water, add one tablespoon of bicarbonate of soda, and allow to soak.

Small bowls of bicarbonate of soda placed in your fridge and food cupboards will absorb any unpleasant odours. Sprinkle it in the bottom of your kitchen bin for a similar effect.

Rub away scuffs such as heel marks from hard floors with a damp cloth and bicarbonate of soda.

To remove stinky stains from the loo, sprinkle bicarbonate of soda into the toilet bowl, add vinegar, and wipe clean with paper towels and elbow grease.

Lemon juice – a natural bleaching agent and disinfectant. Freshly sliced lemon and bottled concentrated juice are equally effective.

Rub lemon juice with salt to clean copper and brass. Rinse with water.

Bleach wooden chopping boards by applying lemon juice. Leave to sit overnight, then rinse thoroughly.

Use lemon juice to remove stains such as blood, grass, pet accidents and mildew.

Soda water – an excellent cleaner for red wine and coffee spills on carpet. Keep a bottle handy for emergencies. Absorb the moisture by covering with a white towel (the dye on coloured towels may transfer) and treading on it.

Toilet soap – keep a bar handy – it will remove a multitude of marks from upholstery and fabrics.

Make a general all-purpose cleaner by mixing together 500ml of water, two tablespoons of lemon juice, half a teaspoon of washing-up liquid, a tablespoon of bicarbonate of soda and a teaspoon of borax in a spray bottle. Shake well and apply to any hard surface.

Store home-made cleaners in spray bottles, remembering to label them clearly for future use.

All these natural mixes are tried and tested. Never mix commercial cleaning products as the combination can create toxic fumes.

Mouldy old homes

It's not a pretty sight, is it, dear – green furry growth spreading in corners, around window frames and at the back of cupboards. Mould and mildew will happily form when there are high levels of humidity and lack of adequate ventilation. Mould can also make you sick. Mould spores become airborne and that's when the trouble starts, aggravating asthma and respiratory problems. The older folk and little ones are especially at risk, because their immune systems are more vulnerable.

TO PREVENT MOULD FORMING

1 Keep your home clean and dry, and well ventilated.

2 Keep humidity low by opening windows, or fitting extractor fans and airbricks in rooms with high levels of moisture such as bathrooms and kitchens.

3 When drying washing inside, open a window to allow the moisture to escape, which helps reduce humidity levels.

4 When using the tumble drier, keep a window open to allow ventilation.

5 Open the bathroom window after bathing and showering to allow fresh air in, and remove moisture-laden air. Alternatively leave the extractor fan running for a while. When you take a bath, run the cold water first, followed by the hot. This cuts down condensation substantially.

6 Keep an eye open for tell-tale damp patches caused by leaking plumbing, or damaged roofs. Have the problem attended to as soon as possible before dampness damages the building, and your health.

Extra activities in the bedroom

If you suffer from asthma, or from an allergic reaction to dust, please pay extra care in the bedroom. You spend up to a third of your life in here, so make the stay a pleasant one. Follow these simple tips and you'll keep dust – and therefore dust mites – at bay.

Open a window each day, even if only for a few minutes. The fresh air reduces the density of allergens in the room. It also helps reduce the moisture content of the air, which builds up as we sleep. It is this high humidity that dust mites thrive in.

Turn back the bedcovers each morning and let the undersheet and mattress breathe. The flow of air will allow the moisture that we perspire during the night – up to half a litre per person – to evaporate.

Cover mattresses, pillows and duvets with anti-allergen covers. These prevent skin flakes getting into the bedding, thus keeping down levels of dust mites. Alternatively look for hypo-allergenic fillings and labels on pillows and duvets when you replace them.

Change the bedlinen at least once a week. Use sheets you can wash at 60°C – this hotter temperature will not only remove the allergens but will also kill the dust mites.

Wash duvets, pillows and bedroom curtains regularly. Check the labels for washing instructions. Dry-cleaning will kill mites but it won't remove the allergens, and it may also leave irritating residue from dry-cleaning solvents.

Vacuum the room at least twice a week, and the mattress and under the bed at least once a month.

Filled soft toys can harbour allergens. If your child is sensitive, limit the number of these playthings, and wash them regularly.

So how clean is your house?

There, doesn't that feel better, dear? Now you have a lovely clean home, sweet smelling, everything in its place, beds made, mirrors gleaming, taps shining and carpets freshly vacuumed. You can put your feet up and relax, but please don't go thinking it's done forever – the war against dirt is never over, it just takes a breather.

We've met some lovely people since *How Clean Is Your House?* first appeared on TV. Cleaning doesn't seem to be women's work anymore, does it? Children, teenagers, young men and even professional city types all seem to be donning their rubber gloves and scrubbing and polishing with new vigour. Is it our imagination or does Britain now smell just a little bit of vinegar?

Keep cleaning now, dears – you'll feel better for it, your loved ones will thank you and your home will absolutely sparkle. Next time anyone asks you How Clean Is Your House?, just you tell them – Kim and Aggie would be proud of me!

index

acknowledgements

acknowledgements

Kim and Aggie would like to express huge thanks to Jerry Foulkes ('What a clean young man') and Stephanie Harris ('Dear Steph, such a clever girl and what a joy to work with') without whom the television series and the writing of this book would not have been possible.

We are indebted to the combined genius of Daisy Goodwin and Ben Frow whose original conversation provided the chance remark 'How clean is your house?' This set us off, cleaning up Britain, with millions of viewers following our weekly progress with glee and astonishment.

Thanks also to those nice people at Penguin, Kate Adams and John Hamilton, for being such big admirers of the show, who, along with Cat Ledger, saw the potential to turn it into a book. And not forgetting Mark Read, our fantastic photographer.

Kim would like to thank her ever loyal hubby Pete (he's the best in the world, my Pete, I'm ever so lucky) and kitty Daisy for holding the fort while she was away attending to other people's needs. Kim is indebted to Jane Urquhart at Greycoat Placements, for thinking of her when asked to name Britain's top cleaner.

Aggie wants to thank her husband Matthew for his unstinting support and sons Rory and Ewan for not being too embarrassed by Mum's new-found infamy. Thanks also to friends and colleagues at Good Housekeeping for their encouragement, generosity and patience.

Of course none of this would be possible without the entire How Clean Team: Jenny Freilich, Harry Beney, Simon Bisset, Lynda Maher, Jules Seymour, Kate Shepherd, Shaheen Gould, Nan Whittingham, Caroline McCool, Victoria Coker, Katie Attwood, Hannah Brownhill, Janet Chamberlain, Nina Somers, Tim Compton, James Lloyd, Dave Holland, Paul Singleton, the Knights, Paul Copley, Hugo and Vicky at Huge, Al Collingwood and all at Fusion.